EDUCATION IN A COMPETITIVE AND GLOBALIZING WORLD

MOBILE LEARNING (M-LEARNING) CONCEPTS, CHARACTERISTICS, METHODS, COMPONENTS. PLATFORMS AND FRAMEWORKS

EDUCATION IN A COMPETITIVE AND GLOBALIZING WORLD

Additional books in this series can be found on Nova's website under the Series tab.

Additional e-books in this series can be found on Nova's website under the e-book tab.

EDUCATION IN A COMPETITIVE AND GLOBALIZING WORLD

MOBILE LEARNING (M-LEARNING) CONCEPTS, CHARACTERISTICS, METHODS, COMPONENTS. PLATFORMS AND FRAMEWORKS

MOHAMED SARRAB

New York

Copyright © 2015 by Nova Science Publishers, Inc.

All rights reserved. No part of this book may be reproduced, stored in a retrieval system or transmitted in any form or by any means: electronic, electrostatic, magnetic, tape, mechanical photocopying, recording or otherwise without the written permission of the Publisher.

For permission to use material from this book please contact us:
nova.main@novapublishers.com

NOTICE TO THE READER

The Publisher has taken reasonable care in the preparation of this book, but makes no expressed or implied warranty of any kind and assumes no responsibility for any errors or omissions. No liability is assumed for incidental or consequential damages in connection with or arising out of information contained in this book. The Publisher shall not be liable for any special, consequential, or exemplary damages resulting, in whole or in part, from the readers' use of, or reliance upon, this material. Any parts of this book based on government reports are so indicated and copyright is claimed for those parts to the extent applicable to compilations of such works.

Independent verification should be sought for any data, advice or recommendations contained in this book. In addition, no responsibility is assumed by the publisher for any injury and/or damage to persons or property arising from any methods, products, instructions, ideas or otherwise contained in this publication.

This publication is designed to provide accurate and authoritative information with regard to the subject matter covered herein. It is sold with the clear understanding that the Publisher is not engaged in rendering legal or any other professional services. If legal or any other expert assistance is required, the services of a competent person should be sought. FROM A DECLARATION OF PARTICIPANTS JOINTLY ADOPTED BY A COMMITTEE OF THE AMERICAN BAR ASSOCIATION AND A COMMITTEE OF PUBLISHERS.

Additional color graphics may be available in the e-book version of this book.

Library of Congress Cataloging-in-Publication Data

ISBN: 978-1-63463-252-2

Published by Nova Science Publishers, Inc. † New York

Dedication

This book is dedicated to:

*The spirit of my grandfather
Mohamed Khalefa Sarrab*

Special person in my life and has special place in my heart.

Acknowledgments

In the name of **Allah**, the Most Gracious and the Most Merciful, I give thanks to Him for supporting me with the strength to complete this book. Without His support, none of this effort would have been possible. This book could not have been possible completed without the recommendations, support and advice of many people.

The idea for this book was generated because of M-learning research project that Dr. Mohamed Sarrab is currently involved with. This research project is funded by The Research Council (TRC) of the Sultanate of Oman: under Grant No: ORG/SQU/ICT/13/006, (www.trc.gov.om). Thanks to The Research Council (TRC) of the Sultanate of Oman for taking a leadership role in innovation in research and for funding this important M-learning project.

Thank you.

Muscat,
Sultanate of Oman, 2014

Mohamed Sarrab

Contents

List of Figures	xiii
List of Tables	xv
SQU, TRC and CIRC	xvii
Feedback	xix
Preface	xxi

1 Introduction — 1
  1.1 Learning Models — 2
  1.2 Book Organization — 5

2 Learning — 9
  2.1 Introduction — 9
  2.2 Traditional Learning — 10
  2.3 Distance Learning — 11
  2.4 Virtual Learning — 13
  2.5 Electronic Learning — 14
  2.6 Ubiquitous Learning — 16
  2.7 Mobile Technology and Learning — 17
  2.8 Summary — 19

3 Mobile Computing — 21
  3.1 Introduction — 21
  3.2 Concept of Mobile Computing — 22
  3.3 Mobile Application Development Platforms — 23
    3.3.1 Iphone OS — 24
    3.3.2 Android — 26
    3.3.3 Symbian — 28
    3.3.4 Windows — 29
    3.3.5 MeeGo — 31

		3.3.6	Plam WebOS	32
		3.3.7	Bada	33
		3.3.8	LiMo	35
		3.3.9	Blackberry	36
		3.3.10	PyS60	37
	3.4	Summary		39

4 Mobile Learning — 41
- 4.1 Introduction — 41
- 4.2 History of M-Learning — 42
- 4.3 Definitions and Theoretical Background of M-Learning — 43
- 4.4 M-Learning Characteristics — 45
- 4.5 M-Learning Methods — 47
  - 4.5.1 Formal M-Learning — 48
  - 4.5.2 Non-formal M-Learning — 49
  - 4.5.3 Informal M-Learning — 49
- 4.6 M-Learning Components — 50
  - 4.6.1 Stakeholders — 50
  - 4.6.2 Mobile Device — 51
  - 4.6.3 Mobile App — 53
  - 4.6.4 Learning Material — 55
- 4.7 Summary — 56

5 M-Learning Requirements — 57
- 5.1 Introduction — 57
- 5.2 Overview of M-Learning Tools — 58
- 5.3 M-Learning Requirements — 59
- 5.4 Pedagogical and Educational — 61
  - 5.4.1 Social and Cultural — 62
  - 5.4.2 Business and Economic — 63
  - 5.4.3 Technical and Quality — 64
  - 5.4.4 Availability — 65
  - 5.4.5 Quick Response — 66
  - 5.4.6 Flexibility — 66
  - 5.4.7 Scalability — 67
  - 5.4.8 Connectivity — 67

		5.4.9	Performance	68
		5.4.10	Reliability	68
		5.4.11	Functionality	68
		5.4.12	Usability	69
		5.4.13	Efficiency	69
		5.4.14	Maintainability	69
		5.4.15	User Interface	69
		5.4.16	Security	70
	5.5	Summary		72

6 Frameworks — 75
   6.1 Introduction — 75
   6.2 An Overview of M-Learning Frameworks — 76
   6.3 Existing Approaches of M-Learning Frameworks — 77
   6.4 Summary — 90

7 M-Learning in Education — 93
   7.1 Introduction — 93
   7.2 The Use of M-Learning in Education — 94
   7.3 Basic Schools — 94
   7.4 Higher Education Providers — 95
   7.5 Research and Training Centers — 96
   7.6 Characteristics of M-Learning in Education — 97
   7.7 Technical Barriers — 98
   7.8 Non-technical Barriers — 98
   7.9 Summary — 100

8 Summary — 101
   8.1 Summary of the Book — 101
   8.2 Open Issues and Future Direction — 103

References — 107

Index — 131

List of Figures

1.1	Learning Models Development.	4
3.1	Mobile Computing Components.	23
3.2	Apple.	25
3.3	Android.	27
3.4	Symbian.	28
3.5	Windows.	30
3.6	MeeGo.	31
3.7	Palm WebOS.	32
3.8	Bada.	34
3.9	LiMo.	35
3.10	BlackBerry.	37
3.11	Python.	38
4.1	An Overview of M-learning Stakeholders.	51
5.1	M-learning as a subset of E-learning.	59
5.2	M-learning Requirements Dimensions.	60
5.3	Pedagogical and Educational Requirements.	62
5.4	Social and Cultural Requirements.	63
5.5	Business and Economic Requirements.	64
5.6	Technical and Software Quality Characteristics.	65
5.7	of M-learning Requirements for Security.	70
6.1	Laurillard's conversational framework.	77
6.2	Ali's Framework of Mobile Learning Systems.	78
6.3	M-learning Design Requirements Framework.	78

List of Figures

6.4	M-learning Framework.	79
6.5	The FRAME Model.	80
6.6	The MOTEL framework.	81
6.7	M-learning Framework for an Analog Electronics Course.	82
6.8	Phases in Creation of the Current Version Mobile Learning Curriculum.	83
6.9	Standard Hierarchical Framework.	84
6.10	The main criteria of proposed M-Learning framework.	84
6.11	Mobile Device Constraints.	85
6.12	Quality of services and applications.	86
6.13	Learners Requirements.	87
6.14	Four types of mobile learning: A pedagogical framework.	87
6.15	Architecture of Opencast Mobile Learning System (OMLS).	88
6.16	ADL Mobile Learning Framework.	89
6.17	Mobile Learning in Context Framework.	90
6.18	Main Components of Comprehensive M-learning Framework.	91

List of Tables

4.1	An overview of M-learning definitions	44
6.1	An overview of M-learning frameworks	76

SQU, TRC and CIRC

Sultan Qaboos University (SQU) is the realization of the promise announced by His. Majesty Sultan Qaboos Bin Said during the 10th anniversary of Oman's National Day in 1980.Construction started in 1982. In accordance with the Royal Directives of His Majesty, The University Engineering, Agriculture, Education and Science. Then it followed by College of Arts, Commerce and Economics, Law and Nursing. Sultan Qaboos University aspires to be an outstanding center of science and research characterized by innovation and creativity, a university that is a source of Omani pride.

The Research Council (TRC) has developed a National Research Strategy for Oman which is linked to the Sultanate's overall development plans and, like them, has the clear goal and vision of improving all aspects of life in Oman. It sets up a system that is responsive to national and international needs; fosters innovation and scientific excellence; and makes a positive contribution to society. The main themes of the Strategy are: building greater research capacity; achieving research excellence in fields of national importance; creating a supportive environment for research; disseminating knowledge and utilizing academic research.

Communication and Information Research Center (CIRC) is located at Sultan Qaboos University and is one of the many research centers established in the office of deputy vice chancellor post-graduate studies and research. CIRC is seeks is to be recognized nationally and internationally as the center of excellence for Research and Development in Telecommunication and Information Technologies. It aims to promote and enhance information and communication technologies through applied research and development, consultancy and training. These goals will be achieved by developing and maintaining strong relationships with industry, ministries, and educational organizations, nationally and internationally.

Feedback

I greatly value my readers opinions and would appreciate information about any mistakes the reader might encounter in the text or technical portions of this book.

Please contact me in case of concerns at: sarrab@squ.edu.om
Readers comments will enable me to improve the quality of the text greatly. Thanks in advance for any feedback or suggestions you as a reader can provide

Mohamed Sarrab

Preface

Welcome to my textbook!

The widespread use of mobile technologies, both hardware and software, is quickly becoming a prerequisite to support development. This widespread use, combined with improvements in mobile connectivity, has led to increasing interest in the use of mobile devices as learning tools. Distance and electronic learning have proven to be potential approaches, insuring progress in education that reduces the limitations of traditional education systems. Mobile learning (M-learning) represents how best to address a number of traditional, distance, visual and electronic learning challenges, issues and limitations. The opportunity to use mobile devices, such as PDAs, tablets and smart phones, as learning tools, enables innovation and supports students, teachers and decision makers access to digital study materials and personalized assessment.

Much of the work done on the subject of M-learning has taken the form of requirement analysis, design needs and issues and challenges affecting application development. In order to ascertain the current level of knowledge and state of research, this book pinpoints and harnesses the potential factors and gaps in M-learning development and adoption. This book presents different aspects related to M-learning to help readers understand and distinguish the primary characteristics and features of M-learning.

The book begins with an introductory chapter that describes its scope. The second chapter describes the principles of learning and teaching. This is followed by 6 chapters, which describe and discuss mobile computing, different definitions of M-learning and its theoretical background, different M-learning requirements, M-learning frameworks and number of M-learning applications in the field of education. The final chapter highlights M-learning issues and suggests a future direction for M-learning.

Mohamed Sarrab

Chapter 1

Introduction

Objectives

- Motivate the needs of M-learning.
- Highlight the contribution of the book.
- Outline the organization of the book.

Learning concerns the ability to acquire knowledge, and learn behavior or skills. This ability to learn involves the capacity to acquire several types of information over a specific period of time [1]. Learning may occur as structured and externally directed, structured and self-directed, unstructured and self-directed and learning at the point of need. In fact, the human learning process begins innately very early in the pregnancy period [2, 3]. The learning process consists of two main components the learner and the content being learned [4]. Traditional learning (T-learning) and normal education models are formulated based on school classroom setups where instructors provide learning material to students. This learning mechanism depends principally on both the students and their instructors physically participating in an identical learning process. [5]. In the T-learning process it is necessary to bring students together in one classroom, where, their learning needs can be met or discussed. However, in some learning mechanisms, instructors are asked to learn, teach or instruct people in different geographic areas.

In the last 10 years, many education providers have agreed on the benefits of ICT in education. They have developed many ICT strategies to improve the education system. ICT can improve both operational efficiency and the teaching process itself. Using ICT in education can cover a wide range of aspects, and requires development in many areas, such as: infrastructure connectivity and hardware, learning materials, teachers' skills and other technical support. In fact, the necessary infrastructure is already in place in most developed countries, and they have made good improvements in other dimensions. Generally, in recent years countries have been adapting and enhancing their learning and teaching systems using ICT; however, many other countries face barriers when seeking to make this change [6].

Sharing a similar expectation of education quality as that in a classroom-based mechanism, learners might use distance learning (D-learning), electronic learning (E-learning) or mobile learning (M-learning) mechanisms to develop comprehensive learning strategies to meet their different needs. D-learning is an old learning mechanism that emerged in the 1970s with the foundation of open universities. This kind of mechanism enabled students to interact with their instructors from their own location, working at their own pace. Subsequently, in the 1980s the Internet gained in popularity, such that E-learning became the remote learning mechanism of choice. This learning technique supported students and instructors interactions, via text, audio or video [7].

There was a global information technology, communication and mobile revolution that caused a noticeable shift from desktop to mobile devices. Mobile and communications technology are changing modes of interaction, discussion, learning, working and accessing information. Mobile technologies have become an effective and easy source of information in our modern lives. Mobile devices offer cheaper methods of Internet access, compared with desktop computers [8, 9, 10]. Currently, tablet PCs allow mobile internet connections with a functionality that is greater than or equal to desktop PCs. In 2011, Horizon reported that by 2015 80% of internet users will be able to access the internet through mobile devices.

1.1. Learning Models

As information and communication technologies continue to improve, M-learning and aim to support learners to access their learning materials using portable or handheld devices at anytime, and anywhere. Each of these learning mechanisms has its own strengths and weaknesses. However, for learners to achieve an enhanced learning performance, they must first understand different types of learning mechanisms. D-learning, E-learning and M-learning provide the content, methods and mechanisms to reduce the limitations of T-learning. M-learning refers to the use of laptops, mobile handheld devices, PDAs and tablet PC technologies, as applied during the learning process. M-learning is an extension of E-learning, in which mobile devices are supported with wireless technologies [11]. In fact, the use of M-learning has been growing rapidly over the last five years, improving fast in developing countries, and those that have seen the fastest improvements in mobile technology (i.e. Canada). The growing use of mobile, information and communication technologies has provided new possibilities for learning and teaching processes, especially in the area of continuing learning for mobile workers [12].

M-learning is considered to be the third learning wave, following on from the second wave, desktop computers, and mainframes as the first wave. The strongest argument supporting the M-learning approach is its availability and ease of access, in which accessing learning content using mobile devices appears to be much easier than when using desktop computers. Despite the huge number of desktops available all over the world, people do not enjoy using them. In most cases, schools and other education providers are offering different computer facilities, although many of their practical labs are being equipped with desktop computers. However, most of these are remote corner labs on campuses, and students struggle to gain access as they are often in use by other students, or used for classes. The distribution of mobile devices is five times higher than that of desktop PCs [13].

In contrast, many students at higher education institutions carry mobile devices that support web access. Most higher education students use mobile and portable devices widely, to access different web pages and send email messages between classes and fill waiting time [14]. Students wish to be allowed to regularly use some of this wasted time, by supporting mobile technology use outside the classroom. In fact, currently, higher education students are rarely asked to complete school work using mobile devices. Indeed, most colleges and universities explicitly prohibit the utilization of mobile technology inside the classrooms. Students sometimes use their mobile devices and web browsers for information searches during study lectures. Other students might use their mobile devices to find translations in bilingual dictionaries, and others might use their mobile cameras to photograph a study board or record power point display slides.

Thus, modern mobile devices can be used as an educational platform. Because, modern mobile devices offer adequate support for standard Internet technologies and are easily accessed by students who get their required knowledge using modern mobile and communication technologies, which are techniques and methods integrated in M-learning. M-learning changes students' learning processes, encouraging them to be more flexible, motivated and interactive. There are possibilities for M-learning integration into existing E-learning systems, which make it easy to remain in touch with most advances made in the teaching system [15].

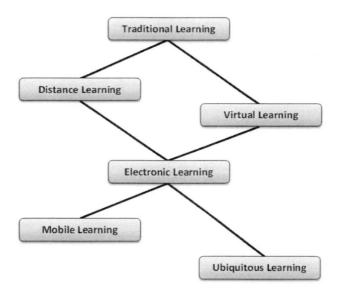

Figure 1.1. Learning Models Development.

This book introduces and evaluates all M-learning related aspects, covering traditional learning, distance learning, virtual learning, electronic learning and ubiquitous Learning. Meanwhile, all aspects of mobile technology and learning are extensively addressed in the context of mobile computing and M-learning, including mobile operating systems, M-learning characteristics, methods, components, requirements and frameworks. Therefore, this book contributes to the body of knowledge by:

- Offering an extensive review of all aspects related to M-learning.
- Studying different kinds of mobile operating systems.

- Discussing different technical and non-technical requirements.
- Analysing all M-learning components and frameworks.
- Exploring the use of M-learning in education.

1.2. Book Organization

The previous sections have provided an overview of the book's scope. The book is made up of a collection organized into chapters:

- **Chapter 2** this chapter provides an introduction to the principles of learning and teaching. It begins by providing an introduction to traditional learning (T-learning) and discusses its methods and components. It then introduces the notion of distance learning (D-learning) and highlights the different advantages and challenges associated with it. It also explores the visual learning (V-learning) concept and discusses its different forms, including computer-based, internet-based, remote instructor online, blended learning and facilitated V-learning. The chapter also introduces different meanings and interpretations of Electronic learning (E-learning) and highlights various advantages. Is also discusses the meaning of ubiquitous learning (U-learning) and discovers unique characteristics. The chapter also focuses on the relationship between mobile technology and different approaches to learning.

- **Chapter 3** this chapter provides a general overview of mobile computing and discusses the main aspects of mobility, including user mobility and device portability. The focus of this chapter is on mobile application development platforms. This chapter begins with an introduction to mobile computing and its main components, mobile communication, mobile hardware and mobile software. It then discusses different mobile application development platforms, including the most well-known mobile operating systems: Iphone OS, Android, Symbian, Windows, Meego, Plam WebOS, Bada, LiMo, Blackberry and PyS60.

- **Chapter 4** begins with a brief history and theoretical background to describe M-learning. It discusses different M-learning definitions and theoretical backgrounds. It starts by presenting a general overview of M-learning characteristics, i.e. portable, simple to use and learn, interactive, context sensitive, flexible, collaborative, privacy, expediency, individualistic, pervasive and accessible. The chapter discusses different M-learning Methods, such as formal, non-formal and informal M-learning methods. The end of the chapter presents the four main M-learning components to be considered when dealing with M-learning systems, including learner, mobile device, learning material and different mobile app e.g. native, web and hybrid apps.

- **Chapter 5** provides an overview of M-learning tools. It discusses different M-learning requirements. It introduces four different requirements of M-learning applications, discussing pedagogical and educational M-learning requirements and diverse characteristics, including learning theories, instructional design models, learning material quality, learning material completeness, learning material presentation, learning material organization and learner support. It also discusses social and cultural M-learning requirements, such as interaction, acceptability, visibility, sociability, attitude and intellectual property. The chapter discusses different businesses and economic M-learning requirements such as cost, feasibility and cost-effectiveness. The chapter also explores various technical and quality requirements including availability, speed of response, flexibility, scalability and security. Covers different important characteristics such as completeness, data integrity, privacy, confidentiality and information flow control.

- **Chapter 6** describes M-learning frameworks and demonstrates how M-learning frameworks are built in order to support different education providers to implement M-learning in their existing or future curricula. This chapter delivers an overview of existing M-learning frameworks, and introduces different components of M-learning frameworks. It discusses the development and adoption aspects of different M-learning frameworks, including the conversational framework for the effective use of learning technologies, a framework for M-learning systems based on educational component, a design requirements framework for M-learning environments, M-learning: a framework and evaluation, a model for framing M-learning, MOTEL: an M-learning framework for Geo-Tagging and explorations of sites for learning, M-learning framework for an analog electronics course, MLCF: the M-learning curriculum framework, hierarchical framework for evaluating success factors of M-learning, a pedagogical framework for M-learning: categorizing educational applications of mobile technologies into four types, an Opencast M-learning framework for enhancing learning in higher education and ADL M-learning framework, mobile learning: not just another delivery method.

- **Chapter 7** this chapter discusses a number of M-learning applications in the education field and identifies their main requirements. It discusses the use of different M-learning applications in education, including the number of education and training providers, higher education providers, training and research centers, and basic schools. The main characteristics of M-learning applications, as designed for use in higher education are also discussed. The chapter also focuses on different technical and non-technical factors that might affect the development, adoption and dissemination of M-learning applications.

- **Chapter 8** the final chapter summaries the book's content, highlights M-learning open issues and suggests a future direction for M-learning.

Chapter 2

Learning

Objectives

- Provide an introduction to T-learning principles.
- Give an overview of D-learning, V-learning and E-learning.
- Discuss the use of mobile technology in different learning mechanisms.

2.1. Introduction

This chapter introduces the principles of learning and teaching. This chapter is divided into five sections. Section 2.2 provides an introduction to traditional learning (T-learning) and discusses its methods and components. Section 2.3 introduces the notion of distance learning (D-learning) and highlights its different advantages and challenges. Section 2.4 introduces visual learning (the V-learning concept) and discusses its different forms, including Computer-Based, Internet-Based, Remote Instructor Online, Blended Learning and Facilitated V-learning. Section 2.5 provides an introduction to the different meanings and interpretations of Electronic learning (E-learning) and highlights its various advantages. Section 2.6 presents the meaning of ubiquitous learning (U-learning) and discusses its characteristics. Section 2.7 discusses the relation between mobile technology and different learning approaches. This section focuses on how mobile technologies are used in learning to promote interactive learning activities and increase learners' motivation.

2.2. Traditional Learning

The concept of theoretical learning concerns the relationship between variables that might effect individual behavior, whilst the concept of teaching focuses on the use of theoretical learning variables to help students achieve their educational objectives. Generally, learning is a process rather than a product that can be produced and involves a change in behavior, beliefs, knowledge or attitudes. However, rather than being an action done to students, learning is instead an action or something students do. It is surprising that most researchers are very rarely explicit about the meaning of the term learning. However, [16] stated that some articles and books have defined learning as a change in behavior due to achieved learning experience. This in fact is a very simple definition of learning where it is defined as a function that changes learners' behavior according to their experiences. Others have claimed that such a basic definition of learning is unsatisfactory [17, 16, 2].

The term learning was referred to by [18] as the changes in behavior that might occur from learner experience; it can also be defined as mechanistic organism changes that occur from experience. [19] argued that both learning definitions are problematic and that a combination of the two should be used, where changes in the organism behaviors of learners are achieved from regularities in the organism's environment. Traditional school learning still uses logical and linguistic teaching as T-learning methods. This limits the range of teaching and learning techniques. Many education providers still use normal classrooms and much repetition, textbook-based learning and students review material via pressurized tests and exams. T-learning uses three main methods in the traditional education system: direct instruction, seatwork and listening and observation. In T-learning, the instructor usually has control of the learning environment and responsibility and power are held by the instructor.

In T-learning, teachers, as knowledge-holders, believe their role is to fill learners with information for learning to occur [20]. In general, the process of T-learning involves three main components, with the learner being anyone learning a subject, skill or seeking knowledge. Learners might be students, trainees or participants. The second T-learning component, education staff, refers to people who provide knowledge to students or deliver instructions in the study area, for example teachers, lecturers, educators, tutors, instructors and trainers. The main responsibilities of education staff are to design and implement instruction techniques to help students reach their educational objectives. The third component comprises the study materials provided by the education staff, including all textbooks, lecture sheets, handwritten notes and other materials used by students.

All the T-learning components described above need to be physically represented in the classroom. Whilst all these T-learning components are important for the learning and education processes, the roles of education and learning staff are very important in the T-learning approaches, as they serve as communicators and providers of study material to the learners [21]. Despite the long history and large amount of research into T-learning, there are many drawbacks and limitations to the current T-learning system, such as the inflexibility of the learning process, which is not available anytime and anywhere [22].T-learning uses some applications of technology to improve teaching, learning and assessment processes.

Learning technology involves the use of multimedia materials, computer-based learning and other communications technology to support the learning process [23]. The idea of Non T-learning approaches come from changing the image of the instructor to someone who knows almost everything to learners having a different level of knowledge to be shared with the instructor's findings. Education staff often teaches their students by selecting and coordinating existing study materials.

2.3. Distance Learning

The marriage between information and communication technologies supports a high degree of interaction between instructors and learners in different and separated geographic areas. The use of network and Internet technologies offers a new learning environment that covers different learning requirements, such as interactions, collaborations and discussion. D-learning is a learning model that delivers education and learning materials for individual learners or students who are not physically present in a T-learning model. Its greater flexibility, widespread availability and easily accessibility are the main reasons to offer instructions using the D-learning model. However, these advantages of D-learning are usually focused on learners separated by time and destination or on learners with disabilities.

D-learning is a model of learning that is typically used at the higher education level, in which learners usually work in the office or at home and communicate with instructors and other learners through the Internet using email, chat rooms, video conferencing, discussion boards, instant messaging, electronic forums and other computer-based learning forms. The Internet is used for most of the D-learning forms to deliver learning materials that are accessible for different students in different locations. Most D-learning forms include computer-based training (CBT), which is used to produce the learners' virtual classroom.

The main advantage of the D-learning model is to keep learners in touch with their instructors and other learners to facilitate discussion and collaboration. D-learning is an effective model of learning for reaching adult learners. Moreover, D-learning supports the use of different technologies which act as tools that assist learning, for example TV, DVDs, discussion ports, online conferencing and printable material. However, web-based learning is usually the first form of learning for many D-learning models [5, 24]. In fact, the rapid development of ICT makes computing resources accessible to all learners. Instructors and learners face the following challenges in typical D-learning courses:

- Blind instructor or learners' need to use a text-to-speech software tool and a speech synthesizer.

- Learners with limited vision need special software tools to enlarge text on the screen.

- Standard printed materials may also be inaccessible to learners with limited vision.

- Some D-learning forms use real-time chat communication for their courses. In this case, learners use synchronous communication, which is difficult for some learners who cannot communicate quickly.

- Web pages for the D-learning model need to be tested with different computer operating systems, platforms and web browsers.

- The televised or video presentation used in the D-learning model should focus on learners who have hearing impairments [25, 26].

- D-learning has two types of delivery forms: synchronous and asynchronous. Synchronous D-learning needs the simultaneous participation of all learners and instructors. Synchronous D-learning supports learners' interaction in real-time, using different types of interaction, including interactive Internet chat, web conferencing, and teleconferencing.

- Asynchronous D-learning does not involve all learners and instructors simultaneously. Learners are not required to be present at the same time and location. Rather, learners may select their own learning time and access the required learning materials and instructors. Asynchronous D-learning is more flexible and widely used than synchronous instruction.

2.4. Virtual Learning

Modern computing devices and Internet technology are transforming the learning process. This emerging education paradigm is referred to as virtual learning or digital learning. V-learning has the potential to improve the teaching ability of instructors and to improve learners' achievements. V-learning uses the Internet and software applications, or both, to deliver instruction to learners. This minimizes the need for instructors and learners to share a study place. V-learning does not include the increasing use of discussion ports, e-mail messages or online forums to enable instructors to provide better interaction with learners and their parents regarding learners' learning progress. V-learning includes the following forms:

- Computer-Based: in this form of V-learning the instructions are not provided by the instructor, as in T-learning methods, but instead via a software application installed on a local server or computer. The learning software application can frequently customize the learning material as suitable for specific learner needs.

- Internet-Based: The concept of Internet-based instruction is similar to computer-based instruction, but the learning software application that provides the learning instruction is delivered using the Web.

- Remote Instructor Online: Instructions are provided by the instructor, who is not physically present with the learners. The instructor communicates with the learner through the Internet, using online video, online discussion ports and e-mail.

- Blended Learning: or hybrid learning combines the traditional classroom with any form of online education, such as traditional face-to-face instruction directed by the instructor, with Internet-based, computer-based or remote instructor online instruction.

- Facilitated V-learning: This is Internet-based, computer-based or remote instructor online instruction that is supplemented by a human as learning facilitator. Unlike in blended learning, the facilitator is not the director. Instead, the facilitator assists the learning process by providing tutoring or additional supervision. This facilitator can be present with the learner or interact remotely using the Web or any other form of electronic communication.

V-learning can be grouped into broader categories:

- Online Learning: includes any form of instruction over the Internet, such as Internet-based instruction, remote instructor online instruction and blended learning and facilitated virtual learning.

- Full-Time Online is an online learning category without regular face-to-face facilitator or instruction, and may be Internet-based or only use a remote instructor. Full-Time Online might include some occasional interaction with human instructors and facilitators.

V-learning provides form of immediate instructor support and feedback [27, 28].

2.5. Electronic Learning

The E-learning approach began in the early 1960s with the Programmed Logic for Automated Teaching Operations (PLATO) project. In the 1970s, the e-learning approach was supported by another project called Time-shared Interactive, Computer-Controlled Information Television (TICCIT). In the 1990s, the e-learning model encompassed all types of electronic-supported teaching and learning [29, 11]. E-learning refers to the use of electronic services in the learning process. In some cases, it is termed 'online learning or online courses'. The e-learning or online learning model is an approach concerned with knowledge or skills development through Internet technologies. As the use of the e-learning model helps students continue learning even though they are not physically present in the classroom, learning activities can thus be adjusted to be flexible around the times when students are available [10]. The E-learning model was originally intended to enable students to learn independently.

A different meaning and interpretation of the E-learning concept mainly defines an explicit association between learners and the digital environment, which refers to the use of computer applications for pedagogical or learning management purposes [30]. [31] described E-learning as the involvement of learning delivery and administration via computer and network technologies to support learners in their performance and development. [32] described E-learning as the use of internet technologies to provide wide set of solutions to enhance learners' knowledge and performance. [33] stated that E-learning is the use of the multimedia and network technologies to enhance learning quality. [34] described E-learning as the implementation of the learning process via a communication system that takes advantage of modern IT, using computer and web-based learning, virtual classrooms and other collaboration between digital services.

In general, e-learning can be defined as the use of all technological and communication support for the learning process, in which E-learning is recognized as computer-aided instruction or web-based training. E-learning is a learning model that utilizes a network such as LAN, WAN or the Internet as a technique to deliver and facilitate learning services. E-learning supports learning anywhere and at any time, as long as learners are connected to the network. The Internet enables E-learning to become state-of-the-art for D-learning all over the world. Using different forms of E-learning, learners can learn at their personal level and according to their ability. This model of learning contrasts with the T-learning concept, which requires learners to be physically present in the classroom or to use self-study material such as textbooks, video, CDs and DVDs.

E-learning has the potential to change our current education and learning process to be more effective and interactive due to the fact that E-learning supports learners' interaction with instructors and enables them to access the required study materials [35, 36]. Computers, satellite transmission, audio and video are used as technology services to support E-learning implementation. E-learning requires some technological infrastructure to exist in order to provide required learning services, such as computers, networks and other appropriate technologies.

E-learning provides many advantages of Internet-based services and facilities, for example multimedia, telecommunication and interactivity faster and more cheaply. These advantages enable e-learning system providers to provide an effective learning system that delivers learning activities in the form of interest, such as games, movies or animation [37]. Moreover, these advantages enable students to continue to learn through discussion or question and answer sessions with both students and instructors through online boards or chatrooms. Whilst the use of E-learning can have an immediate effect on the cost of education and learning processes, it requires a huge investment [21].

2.6. Ubiquitous Learning

A ubiquitous learning (U-learning) environment might detect more context data than E-learning. U-learning contents are defined as learning content that may be transferred to mobile or portable devices through cable or wirelessly and be run in mobile platforms [38, 39]. U-learning is not necessarily bound to the use of mobile devices as learning tools. Whilst it can rely on mobile devices, stationary personal computers, photocopiers or televisions can also be used. Generally, U-learning is enabled by an environment that can be accessed in different situations and contexts. As reported by Van't Hooft et al. (2007), U-learning includes learning in an environment in which all learners have access to different digital devices and services, involving computers connected to the Internet and mobile computing devices, whenever and wherever they are needed [40]. U-learning is a subset of e-learning that is individualized, enables collaborative work, expands access and able to provide learners with instant feedback. U-learning helps learners to access the learning environment anywhere, compared to only working on stationary desktop computers. One of the major differences between learning somewhere on a stationary desktop computer and using mobile devices as a learning tool is the learning context [41]. The following are the main characteristics of U-learning:

- Permanency: learning materials and work assignments are never lost unless learners delete them for another purpose. Moreover, all the learning processes are recorded every day.

- Accessibility: the learning process involved is learning using a self-directed process in which learners have access to their data, files or other study materials from anywhere.

- Immediacy: using U-learning irrespective of location enables learners to access and retrieve the information required immediately, enabling them to quickly solve problems.

- Interactivity: using U-learning, knowledge becomes more widely available as experts are more reachable. Learners are able to interact with experts, instructors, or friends in the form of synchronous or asynchronous communication.

- Adaptability: the use of U-learning can enable learners to obtain the correct information during the learning process at the right place using the right method.

2.7. Mobile Technology and Learning

Mobility, coupled with ease of access, flexibility of use and the integration of software application and media, enables learners work more continuously across school, work or the home. Mobile and communication technologies are an increasingly very useful aspect of learning systems. Younger generations have widely accepted the use of modern mobile technologies and young users have grown up with mobile devices. It is now obvious that the variety of mobile technologies hold learners' attention. Learners are engaged in gaining knowledge using different features (auditory, visual, kin-esthetic) [42, 43]. The outcome of different research studies [42, 44, 45] have shown that the use of mobile technology facilities helps young learners retain their knowledge and skills. Consequently, model software developers often target and try to design mobile applications that will be accepted and embraced by younger users.

The use of mobile technologies has become very common and supportive of the learning process in the context of M-learning. Learners and tutors became gradually more mobile as time goes on, using mobile devices as learning assistance tool [46]. However, the software application for mobile platforms might be designed for several different purposes. One of these purposes involves the use of learning or administrative tools to help learners in their study and tutors in their work. The widespread use of learning systems and mobile technologies indicates the importance of designing and developing wireless and mobile learning applications [47, 48, 49]. Wireless and mobile learning applications provide different learning methods that can be used by tutors and learners to obtain knowledge, stay connected with other learners, engage in discussions with tutors and access instructional resources [50].

Ambient Wood is a project established in 2004 to provide an application to enable students to share their field trip learning experience within a classroom context using mobile devices. The main objectives of this research project were to determine what type of digital materials was required, how and when to offer and deliver materials, and how students should interact with the materials. The project results demonstrate that students were able to use their mobile device to display and share information about their field trip. Students were also able to obtain desired information based on their detected location. This project was successfully designed to avoid students becoming overloaded with too much digital information at once that may affect their interaction with each other. At its conclusion, the project demonstrated that mobile applications can provide a new form of student collaboration and interaction [51].

The Personal Learning Organizer project was established in 2007. It was designed to act as a guide for system requirements to support university students by providing location awareness. Ryu et al. used an interview with ten university students to collect the information needed for the project to identify which design features, material, tasks and learning context should be provided. The outcome of this research indicated that students had different learning requirements when using their mobile devices depending on their university level [52].

The widespread of mobile technologies may enable many professionals and learners in the education community to see learning using mobile devices as a simple extension of E-learning courses using mobile devices. Many training developers and education professionals are trying to create new learning content suitable for use in mobile devices, whilst other professionals and developers are trying to convert existing E-learning materials. However, it is very important for the developers of mobile education and learning contents to consider leveraging different mobile platform capabilities such as sensors, camera and GPS [53].

Mobile technologies are used in learning to promote interactive learning activities and to increase learners' motivation. The motivation of learners will depend on their level of engagement in different learning activities that involve the improved use of new technologies [54, 55]. It is thus desirable to develop some instructional implications on how these technologies can be best adapted to the conventional learning activities. [56] discussed how the use of new technologies in learning activities can enable learners to use mobile devices to improve access to the evaluation system and learning resources, for example enabling learners to look at information anywhere and any time. New changes in the learning and teaching processes, for example modifying learning contents tailored to the individual learner needs or offering an effective context-awareness system that reacts to learners needs, must also be considered.

The establishment of relationships between business targets and academic goals, for example enabling learners to use mobile devices for study and any other educational purposes, supports the use of mobile technologies with E-learning infrastructures to enhance learners' interaction. [57] provided a type of technical and pedagogical approach for supporting different learning activities in the classroom or outside the school. The approach uses PDAs equipped with GPS cards for recording bird observations. Another approach, JAPE-LAS [58], helped students learn polite Japanese expressions, which is a context-aware language learning system. [59] evaluated a mobile learning organizer that designed for graduate students.

2.8. Summary

This chapter has discussed the principles of learning and teaching. The principles of T-learning and its related methods and components were introduced. An overview of D-learning was given and its different advantages and challenges highlighted. Different forms of V-learning were also discussed. This chapter also introduced different meanings and interpretations of E-learning and highlighted its different advantages. The meaning of U-learning and its characteristics were discussed. Finally, the relation between mobile technology and different learning approaches were discussed, with more focus on the use of mobile technologies in learning approaches to promote interactive learning activities and to increase learners' motivation.

Chapter 3

Mobile Computing

Objectives

- Provide a general overview of mobile computing.
- Explore the main components of mobile computing.
- Discuss mobile application development platforms.

3.1. Introduction

This chapter provides a general overview of mobile computing and discusses the main aspects associated with mobility, including user mobility and device portability. The focus of this chapter is on mobile application development platforms. The chapter is divided into nine sections. Section 3.2 introduces mobile computing and its main components: mobile communication, mobile hardware and mobile software. Section 3.3 discusses different mobile application development platforms, including the most well-known mobile operating systems: iPhone OS, Android, Symbian, Windows, Meego, Plam WebOS, Bada, LiMo, Blackberry and PyS60. Finally 3.4 provides a chapter Summary.

3.2. Concept of Mobile Computing

Mobile computing is defined by [60] as a small computing component, which is added to many computing environments. Mobile computing concerns with software application performance and issues arise in response to mobile users movements. [61]. The main concern with mobile computing is the ability to develop mobile software applications that can run successfully on small battery-powered electronic tools, equipped with wireless network connectivity [62]. Mobile computing encompasses different types of devices and technologies, such as smart phones, netbooks, wireless networks, PDAs, and tablet PCs.

Simply put, any portable electronic device that supports and assists communication and job efficiency and performance is a component of mobile computing. Mobile data communication is a rapidly improving technology that supports mobile users data the sending and transmission of mobile users data from remote locations to others locations, whether remote or fixed. The normal use of mobile phones, e.g. phone calls, text message or music lessons are not involved in any type of mobile computing activities, and the use of laptops and other portable devices without a "home base" connection through a network are not a type of mobile computing [61]. The main aspects of mobility are:

- User mobility: can communicate anywhere, anytime with anyone.

- Device portability: can connect anytime and anywhere to the network.

The high demand for user mobility and device portability creates a requirement for the integration of different types of network, whether wireless or fixed. Mobile computing has three main components:

- Mobile communication (wireless) concerns with network communication issues, connection protocols, and data formats.

- Mobile hardware (device) manages the hardware devices used

- Mobile software (Application) concerned with the mobile application's characteristics and requirements.

The main components of mobile computing are the mobility of the data, and the hardware and software applications. Mobile systems appear to be closely related to traditional distributed systems, but, there are many factors that differentiate them: network connection type, whether permanent or intermittent;

device type, whether fixed or mobile; and static or dynamic execution context. Modern mobile devices possess a broad array of different technologies specifications and features [63].

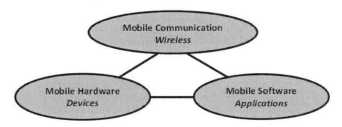

Figure 3.1. Mobile Computing Components.

Many portable and mobile devices have memory capabilities and a processor performance comparable to desktop PCs, with high speed communication abilities making mobile computing the perfect target for research of this nature [11]. The field of mobile computing integrates different application scenarios, such as smart mobile phones, nomadic users, meeting rooms, vehicles, police and fire squad fleets, online conferences, intelligent offices and smart houses, invisible computing, disaster alarm systems, disaster relief, military and games. [64].

3.3. Mobile Application Development Platforms

The application design and implementation of mobile devices differs from the development of desktop PC applications, because of the nature of mobile devices and their context of use. Mobile devices and applications with similar functionalities are not portable from one device to another, and each mobile device requires its own implementation. There are many different mobile applications and development platforms in use. These platforms differ because of mobile operating system incompatibility, development models and communication choices. Therefore, it is a challenge for developers to develop mobile applications that are suitable for a wide variety of mobile devices [65].

Similar to a normal computer operating system, the mobile operating systems is a software platform. Mobile device manufacture is responsible for the choice of mobile device operating system, and the operating system is responsible for specifying the main features and functionalities of the device; e.g. wireless connectivity, text messaging, keyboards, audio, video etc. Mobile operating systems also specify which third-party applications will be used on a device [66]. Mobile operating systems can be clustered into different groups, such as Microsoft, Blackberry, Symbian, Linux and Apple [11]. However, primary competitors in the sphere of mobile operating systems are Apple iOS, Googles Android, BlackBerry and Windows Phone 7. The most well-known mobile operating systems are:

3.3.1. Iphone OS

Apple Inc., which has developed and marketed iOS, which is the iPhone mobile operating system (iPhone m-OS). iOS was initially named iPhone OS but in 2010 it was renamed to reflect the operating system's ability to support any Apple devices. iOS is used as the default operating system for all Apple products including the iPhone, iPad, iPod Touch, Apple TV and similar devices [67]. In fact, iOS is a simplified form of the Mac operating system X, hence, it is a Unix type operating system. Apple provided it as a proprietary operating system. It involves four different abstraction layers, Touch interface, Media, Core Services and Core Operating System [68].

Apple has provided public Software Development Kit (SDK) for a software development, to enable developers to develop software applications using Objective C as a programming language. Apple SDK enables developers to develop software applications to utilise software and hardware features on commercially available devices, such as multitouch, hardware sensors, audio programming, and 3D transformations. Apple SDK includes Xcode (Source code editor, compiler, graphical debugger, development environment with project management and documentation... etc.), User Interface Builder and iPhone Simulator.

Xcode is an integrated development environment, suitable for developing Mac and iPhone applications. Xcode has been developed to support users to write programs in different languages, i.e. C, C++, Objective C, Python, Ruby and Cocoa. Whereas, Xcode is installed on different types of CoMPLEX computers, and is also available to download from Mac Dev Center. Xcode has a software application framework called Cocoa, which supports Objective-C 2.0 as programming language for Apple applications.

Cocoa is an object-oriented language used for writing native Mac applica-

Figure 3.2. Apple.

tions. It is based on Objective C, which is based on C. Objective C can be compiled to run on different platforms; however, Cocoa has frameworks that are designed to run only on Mac. Apple iOS is currently in a v7.x release, which has introduced a number of new powerful features for use in mobile OS, such as a built-in iMessage (instant messaging client), Siri tool as advanced voice recognition and iCloud as a service for personal cloud storage. Apple provides three levels of app development:

- Tools, concerned with the use of Xcode to build and manage projects.
- Technologies, related to building apple apps that respond to user input.
- Techniques, considering some advantages of design patterns that underlie all apple app development.

Thus, to develop iOS apps, the following are necessary components:

- A Mac machine.
- Xcode.
- iOS SDK.

To begin developing an iOS app, the developer first needs to create a new Xcode project. This comprises different built-in iOS app templates, which can be used for developing common iOS apps styles, such as navigation apps, games and other apps for table view. These iOS app templates have preconfigured source code files and interfaces, to make the developer's work easier. Xcode has everything the developer needs to create and maintain the iOS app, such as organizing the necessary files to create the new app, providing editors for the interface and code features and offering a powerfully integrated debugger.

Xcode enables empty application templates to be built without any code, and run without any additional configurations. The iOS Simulator app is used to build and run the iOS app thats included in Xcode. iOS Simulator has the capability to model different types of apple devices, such as iPhone and iPad, with different screen sizes. Thus, any iOS built app can be run on every apple device. Meanwhile, iOS Simulator starts automatically after Xcode finishes building the project [65, 11]. iPhone OS has some associated issues such as:

- Iphone OS is Apple devices dependent.
- Application is a black box for developers.
- Downloads are dependent on the application's promotion in store.
- The Apple store is the only authorized application distribution channel.
- iPhone OS is a closed source, which means it, is not possible for a developer to change, modify or redistribute the source code.

3.3.2. Android

Android is provided as mobile devices software stack; it comprises three main components: an operating system, middleware and software applications. Android OS is one of the latest operating systems for mobile devices, and was developed by Google and Open Handset Alliance [69]. Android is developed as an open source platform, which is available under open source license. Android is also based on the Linux kernel. The Java programming language is used as a core language to develop on Android platforms. All Android applications will have similar operating system rights and privileges, to enable the use of available functionalities, such as touchscreen, multimedia, GPS, video, acceleration features and camera.

The Android platform supports all applications with equal rights and privileges [70]. Android SDK offers the necessary tools and APIs, using the Java programming language, to develop an application on an Android platform [71].

Figure 3.3. Android.

The Android SDK is a user friendly development environment, which contains a device emulator, memory, performance profiling, debugging tools and an Eclipse IDE plugin. The first release of Android is the Android 1.0 SDK, and was provided by Google at four different architecture levels. These include the operating system, framework for application development, a middle ware with core libraries, a runtime environment and other applications.

Mobile operators control the type of mobile apps and features that can operate on the mobile device, and the use of mobile operator networks is not the same with PCs; where users have complete control of both software and hardware. Google has overcome this limitation by providing its platform as open source and, supporting the freedom to use and run any compatible mobile application by supporting carriers over the globe, as included in the Open Handset Alliance. Android Architecture includes the operating system as a Linux 2.6 kernel, with other device drivers included. Whereas, this architecture layer handles the process and memory management, network stack, device driver model and the security.

C/C++ libraries act as interfaces between kernel/device drivers and the application framework. Android uses a set of basic libraries to provide all possible and available functionality for the core in Java programming language libraries. The libraries support Dalvik Virtual Machine (DVM), as an Android Runtime Engine. DVM relies on the Linux kernel for underlying functionality, e.g. threading and low level memory management. The DVM supports every application to run as a single independent process over its own individual instance of DVM. The layers of application frameworks are fully written in the Java programming language and consist of several components such as Window Manager, Package Manager, Activity Manager, Resource Manager, Telephony Manager, Notification Manager, Location Manager, View System and Content providers. The applications run on top of the application framework layer, which contains details of both the platform supplied and user developed applications. [71, 72].

The rapid development of Android operating system has provided several functionalities, such as more supportive multi-touch, multitasks and double tap zoom. Of these, multi-tasking functionality is one of the most powerful features of Android. Additionally, the appearance of the user interface is modern and provides a clear advantage over touch screen. The android operating system has been developed with the aim of being always on, and the majority of its processing operations are performed online, which makes Android operation system the most suitable choice for developing social communities and cloud computing applications [73, 72]. Android OS has related issues such as:

- Late to market relative to the iPhone
- At least initially, demand was expected to trail iPhone demand

3.3.3. Symbian

Symbian is an operating system and successor to Psion EPOC, which was initially provided by Symbian Ltd. for mobile devices. It supports different associated user interface frameworks and libraries to be used on ARM processors [69]. The Symbian foundation was originally formed in 2008 and consolidated its different user interface platforms; such as UIQ, S60, MOAP(S) to provide the platform as an open source, readily available for study, modification and distribution to anyone, and for any purpose. The use of the Symbian operating system enables binary applications to be installed, and provides different features for hardware devices.

Figure 3.4. Symbian.

Symbian uses an internet protocol networking architecture to support mobile devices, allowing a smooth switch between networks with the best connection types; such as 3G and WiMax. The application developers are supported to use graphics hardware acceleration with Symbian OS native graphics architecture. Symbian offers a graphics composition engine to create overlays and lend transparency to applications by executing different mobile apps as different parallel running processes, offering mobile users more diverse applications contexts, in addition to a 3-D experience. Symbian uses a variant of standard C++ programming language as a native language for its supported devices. Symbian developers are fully supported to use all mobile devices hardware features, while developing mobile applications, although other different runtime environments, like Flash and Java are also supported by Symbian OS [65, 11].

All Nokia devices used Symbian OS until the release of the Lumia 800 at the end of 2011; whereas, new Nokia products no longer support the use of Symbian OS. In fact, in early 2012 the Symbian OS was still the third most popular and widely used operating system. There are different operating systems derived from the Symbian banner, and the Symbian OS itself is advancing to its 10th generation. The newest Symbian version is Nokia Belle 10.1, which was introduced in March 2012. The last release of Symbian OS has many different features, which are not available on any other Symbian OS's; such as deeper NFC integration, pull-down status or notification bar, changes the three home screens to six screens and free form resizable home screen widgets [74]. Symbian OS encounters some problems at present, as detailed below:

- Limited reach in some countries.
- Symbian OS has not been developed for touchscreen devices
- The distribution of applications is more difficult compared with the iPhone app store

3.3.4. Windows

A few years ago Microsoft used different names for the different windows versions it used with mobile devices; whereas, in 2000, Microsoft introduced Windows CE 3.0 as a fundamental OS for the Pocket PC with GUI and other additional applications. In 2003, Microsoft introduced a new release of Windows CE 4.2 as an underlying operating system for Pocket PC. Subsequently, Microsoft started using Windows Mobile devices to refer to the new Pocket PC devices. Windows Mobile was released for different mobile devices, such as Pocket PC, Pocket PC Phone Edition, Smartphones, or phones using windows mobile OS without a touch screen. In 2004, Microsoft provided another updated version of the Windows mobile, called the Windows Mobile 2003 Second Edition.

This was the initial point at which the term Pocket PC was dropped. In 2005 and 2007, Windows Mobile 5 and 6 were introduced respectively. They were built using the Windows CE 5.1 and Windows CE 5.2 as development platforms [75]. Windows mobile is the most recent mobile development platform provided by Microsoft for mobile devices (WM-OS).

Figure 3.5. Windows.

The windows phone is the second oldest mobile operating system, having been released in 2010. In fact, the Windows Phone is the new term used for the Windows Mobile WM-OS; whereas, the WM-OS 6.5 was the most recent version before the release of the Windows Phone. Windows Mobile (WM) is designed to bring PC computing ability to the mobile world. The software development kit (SDK) for the windows mobile provides different tools and libraries for mobile application development, with the Microsoft Visual Studio being its Integrated Development Environment. To simplify the application development process, the software development kit utilised tools, such as the Device Emulator, which simulates application execution in multiple devices.

The software development kit supports .NET Compact Framework. Thus, mobile applications may be developed to run on a Windows Mobile operating system using Microsofts .NET framework. The mobile applications are written in any .NET languages and compiled to byte code, to run on .NET virtual machines with the same version of the OS [69, 65]. Windows Mobile uses similar desktop windows file systems (XP, Windows 7 and 8) to support files being copied or moved between the Windows Mobile and desktop devices. There is only one exception for the communication software; Windows Mobile Device

Center, Microsoft ActiveSync should be configured specifically to convert files into the right application formats of run over Windows Mobile, e.g. Pocket Word [76]. The main issues associated with the Windows Phone OS are as follows:

- Windows Phone OS has a smaller percentage of market share.
- Windows OS experiences less developer enthusiasm than Android and iPhone.
- Windows Phone OS is a closed source, which means it is not possible for a developer to change or modify it.

3.3.5. MeeGo

Intel MeeGo is a Linux-based platform, which is an open source operating system that can run on different computing devices, including smartphones, tablets, Netbooks, and in-vehicle infotainment systems. MeeGo is developed to run on different hardware platforms and supports Intel x86 and ARM processors. MeeGo was originally designed by Intel and Nokia, as a common successor to their Moblin and Maemo OS projects. Whereas, after the release of Nokia N900, and ignoring the use of Symbian OS, Intel, Nokia and Linux foundation provided the idea of developing a new mobile and tablet PC operating system.

Figure 3.6. MeeGo.

The decision to merge Intel and Nokia's two operating system projects, and form MeeGo, was made during the Mobile world congress. In May 2010, the first MeeGo OS release was launched, targeting mobile computing devices, including N900. From the outset, MeeGo provided as many as three different versions, each designed for particular purposes, Netbooks, Mobile devices and Vehicle GPS. The three versions provided different user interfaces, depending on the specifications of the target devices. The main aim of the Linux-based operating system was not only targeting hand held computing devices, but also focusing on interfaces for TVs and other communication platforms and hardware tools used with moving objects. MeeGo delivers a complete open source software stack, starting with a core operating system, progressing to user interfaces, tools and libraries.

MeeGo uses Qt as a cross-platform application framework for application development, and Qt creator as its environment. MeeGo also uses a user interface framework for developers with C++ or QML - CSS & JavaScript like language. Qt Creator is used to support a Qt Integrated Development Environment. The most important feature of MeeGo is its provision as open source; meaning, its users are free to modify and customise any application developed for the MeeGo operating system, under GPL license. MeeGo also uses a Qt interface to provide a better design application. It is extremely simple and easy to use. Finally, because Fedora and Debian are the source of MeeGo, all the basic software available for Linux interfaces can be easily implemented in MeeGo. [77, 78]. MeeGO OS has some related concerns as set out below:

- MeeGo is an open source solution, but it is still difficult to port onto all devices.
- Interfacing with other technologies such as Bluetooth and 3G is difficult.
- Compatibility issues effect the different MeeGo devices.

3.3.6. Plam WebOS

Palm OS was one of the first mobile operating system released in 1996. Palm OS was designed for the Palm PDA and other related devices [Hewlett-Packard 2011b]. The Palm OS is broadly known as a sophisticated, friendly platform for mobile apps developers. Since the first release of the Palm Pilot in 1996, the Palm operating system platform has offered many important business tools for use on mobile devices, as well supporting Internet access and central database manipulation through wireless connections. The HP mobile WebOS is a successor to the Palm operating system. The WebOS is based on a Linux kernel, which was initially introduced in 2009.

WebOS was created to provide users with the necessary capabilities for multitasking and apps intersection, to insure innovative creation and compelling user experiences. Best of all, WebOS is based on simple web creation languages such as HTML, CSS and JavaScript, and supports fast running apps. Moreover,

palm webOS

Figure 3.7. Palm WebOS.

the Plug-In Development Kit (PDK) can also leverage C / C++ source code as a second approach to development [73]. The Palm OS development process is similar to the development of other platforms; e.g. Windows and Motif, but with some differences, due to the drastically different requirements that must be considered by the developer for mobile applications, such as screen space and limited processing power [79, 11].

Palm OS devices face the normal hand-held computing system resource issues, limitations and challenges; such as power consumption, limited processing power because of battery life (the system is always running), processing speed, storage capacity, input digitizer and available Random Access Memory (RAM). The application developer has some specific challenges with the Palm platform, such as the Palm OS application cannot be allocated to a big data structure, since the Palm OS heap memory provided is limited [80]. The issues most related to the Palm OS are:

- Palm OS does not consider concurrent processing.
- The main downside of Palm OS mobile platforms is their lack of multi-tasking.
- Palm's maturity, whereas Palm products are seen as outdated.

3.3.7. Bada

Bada is an open source smartphone platform developed by Samsung Electronics for the mass market. It was initially developed in 2010 for use in a wide range of devices, such as smartphones and tablet computers [81]. Having an open source platform means that mobile devices ship with *Bada* a platform that is accessible to third-party developers for development, building and publishing mobile native applications for mobile users, via the Samsung applications store.

Bada is open source, following the Android philosophy. Because of the kernel configurable architecture Bada, as Samsung defined it, is not an operating system in itself, but a platform enabling users to use the Linux kernel or another real-time OS kernel.

Figure 3.8. Bada.

Smartphone for Everyone is the main vision put forward by *Bada*, with the aim of providing a smartphone experience to more mobile users. Similar to Samsung's devices, which use the Android platform are branded under the Galaxy name, all *Bada* platform devices are branded under the name Wave [82]. To be available to the global market, rather than to a specific geographical market, *Bada* has been designed to deliver more powerful features to support a greater level of configurability for a wide range of hardware. To provide a smarter platform, *Bada* has added some new features, e.g. 3D graphics, an improved user interface, multipoint-touch and a broader application download and installation option.

Moreover, *Bada* devices are usually associated with some kind of sensors, such as face detection, accelerometer and motion sensing [11]. In fact, *Bada* exploit and uses the knowledge and experience gained from Samsung mobile platform's long history. Whereas, Samsung re-uses well proven concepts and supplements them with new and improved features. Other *Bada* features that are worth mentioning are the service integration for APIs into platforms [83, 72]. Services may include social networking, friends lists that support mobile users sharing real-time information with other users, shopping services, commerce APIs, weather services and locations and other points of interest from services. *Bada* has plenty of features, such as sensor support, user interface controls, flash support, and help running applications to provide more interactive execution. In addition, Service-centric features, e.g. SNS integration and in-app-purchasing, help applications to provide a richer and more interactive experience for customers [84]. *Bada* OS has some related concerns such as:

- Bada applications are unable to access the message in-box and receive incoming message notifications because of performance and privacy issues.

- The Bada external sensor API is not open-ended, preventing new technology from being added in the future.

- Bada has multitasking applications issues, because multitasking is possible between native applications and only each Bada application, and the Bada application framework supports the running of only one application at a time.

3.3.8. LiMo

The LiMo platform was created by an industry group called the Mobile Linux handset trade group (LiMo) Foundation in January 2007. The LiMo platform is based on a Linux kernel. The group was comprised of telecommunications providers and handset developers from all mobile phone players such as: handset manufacturers, chip makers, telecom operators, mobile apps developers and others. LiMo is a mobile open source operating system, which aims to create an open hardware-independent Linux-based platform for mobile handheld devices. LiMo replaced a group of previous standards, e.g. Linux Phone Standards (LiPS).

The LiMo Platform was designed to enable mobile handheld device development and deployment, based on a modular architecture and a middleware plugin implemented in either C or C++ and built around the open operating system Linux. The middleware comprises multimedia, network, security, messaging and database frameworks. In addition, developers are free to add other frameworks according to their needs using this architecture. The LiMo Platform has two other components, the Application User Interface Framework (AUIF) and Application Manager Framework (AMF).

The two frameworks are responsible for applications launching and defining the shape of user interface UIs. These frameworks have been used to ensure the application receives user input and is able to render this to the application display. The Application Manager Framework (AMF) for applications download uses a secure package installer. The kernel space includes a Modem interface, device drivers and Linux kernel. [65]. The LiMo operating system is now in its second incarnation, and is called the R2. This second version supports a standard set of different secure APIs for mobile browsers or WRT, such as the Open

Figure 3.9. LiMo.

Mobile Terminal Platform (OMTP) BONDI specification.

The LiMo operating system delivers a secure and consistent interface of Web services to support developers' use across multiple device platforms. Some manufactures use LiMo in their devices, e.g. NEC, LG, Panasonic Mobile Communications, Vodafone and Motorola [73]. The LiMo second version R2 platform supports many technologies, such as personal information management, multimedia, location-based services and especially improved security applications. LiMo uses web technologies CSS, HTML, JavaScript etc., which are similar to WebOS, but have the support of applications running in JVM along with native code [85]. The main issues related to LiMO are:

- LiMo has not been implemented on many different consumer smartphones.

- LiMo as an open platform has its own security issue, such as source code vulnerability to black-hat hackers.

3.3.9. Blackberry

The Blackberry OS was developed as a proprietary software solution (operating system and development platform) for specific mobile devices called BlackBerry smartphones, by a Canadian company called Research-In-Motion (RIM) [86]. The first BlackBerry smartphone was offered to market in 1999 and the most recent BlackBerry 7 device was released in 2011. BlackBerry devices are a type of smartphone designed to have similar functionality to portable media players, internet browsers, PDA, gaming devices, and cameras [82]. Because of the synchronisation options with third party software and their vast communication protocols, Blackberry OS offers a more professional side. Applications are easy for Blackberry developers to create using RIMlets or native J2ME code [11].

The JVM for Blackberry is based on the J2ME implementation on Sun, which is being partly written in assembler, C and C++. The actual Blackberry operating system was provided as native, along with the JVM and all other Java libraries, where the Java libraries internal implementations are also made native. The Blackberry operating system was provided with the support of true multitasking, without any noticeable performance weaknesses. Blackberry operating systems support screen multi-touch in their newer versions, but Flash versions are not supported. The Blackberry operating system is located on the top of JVM as a preinstalled and application development that supports J2ME. Blackberry native implementation is placed in the device firmware,

BlackBerry

Figure 3.10. BlackBerry.

which makes hacking and modification very hard, meaning the operating system does not need to be compiled to the device CPU, and that it also provides an abstraction layer in the hardware for other device hardware functionalities, such as Sound, Radio, Button Control etc. The Blackberry also provides its own applications store, referred to as App World. App world has small number of applications compared with the vast amount of iPhone applications in the Apple store. Blackberry applications are more traditional and integrate weather information and access to web services, with less focus on graphical components [73]. Blackberry OS has some related problems, as outlined below:

- Difficult application distribution.
- Developers recently appear to be shifting to Apple (iPhone).
- Only 6% of market share.

- RIM/hardware dependent.

3.3.10. PyS60

PyS60 is designed to be compatible with the Nokia S60 operating system; it works as an interpreter for the Python programming language [87]. Python was provided by Guido van Rossum to the National Research Institute for Mathematics and Computer Science, Netherlands in 1989. Python has many features, such as easy code reuse; huge standard library and extension with own C/C++ modules. Python is provided as a free and open source, cross platform, with scripting Language, extending and embedding capabilities and access to full phone functionality. Python is an interactive, interpreted, OOPL object-oriented programming language that is often compared with Perl, Scheme, Tcl or even Java. In fact, Python combines remarkable power with a very clear language syntax. Python has classes, exceptions, modules and dynamic data types.

Figure 3.11. Python.

PyS60 can be signed by Nokia, therefore it can be downloaded and installed into different S60 compatible devices. PyS60 enables developers to develop Python applications without the need to be signed, or directly interacting with the operating system. However, the Python applications created have limited functionality, although more device control than the normal applications running on J2ME. All built-in different Python language objects are supported by the S60 platform. However, Python for the S60 environment distribution does not include all the different Python's standards and optional modules in the library to save storage capacity and space in the phone device.

In addition, several excluded library modules work on the S60 Python platform, with no need for any modifications. Some of these modules are comprised in the SDK version but are not actually installed on the phone device. Currently PyS60 is based on Python 2.2.2, which supports different Python Standard Library modules, but also has a few mobile platform specific modules on top, e.g. SMS Messaging, networking, native GUI widgets, Bluetooth, GPRS, GSM Location information. [88, 11]. PyS60 has some limitations such as:

- Thread Support.
- Scalability of User Interface.
- Python interpreter's final cleanup.

3.4. Summary

This chapter has provided a general overview of mobile computing and discussed the main aspects of mobility, including user mobility and device portability. The chapter also described the main mobile computing components, including mobile communication, mobile hardware and mobile software. The chapter also focused on the mobile application development platforms, including the most well-known mobile operating systems Iphone OS, Android, Symbian, Windows, Meego, Plam WebOS, Bada, LiMo, Blackberry and PyS60.

Chapter 4

Mobile Learning

Objectives

- Provide an overview of M-learning history.
- Discuss different M-learning definitions and theoretical Background.
- Give an overview of M-learning characteristics and Methods.
- Present M-learning components.

4.1. Introduction

The aim of this chapter is to provide an overview of M-learning history 4.2 and to discuss the various definitions of M-learning and the theoretical background 4.3. Section 4.4 provides a general overview of the characteristics of M-learning, including the fact that it is portable, simple to use and easy to learn, in addition to being interactive, context sensitive, flexible and collaborative. M-learning also facilitates privacy, enables expediency, and is individualistic, pervasive and accessible. This overview is followed by section 4.5, which examines different M-learning methods, such as formal, non-formal and informal M-learning methods. Finally, section 4.6 explains the four main M-learning components that need to be taken into consideration when dealing with M-learning systems, namely, the learner, the mobile device, the learning material and the mobile app, including native, web and hybrid apps.

4.2. History of M-Learning

In recent years, mobile technologies have evolved from luxury items to become everyday necessities. Whilst the demand for mobile devices has increased, this has meant that the cost of these devices has decreased. With improvements in the capabilities of communication technology, means that mobile devices have started to be used as multi-functional devices capable of performing multiple tasks. The term smartphone usually refers to multi-functional devices; however, there are several portable devices such as the iPod Touch and Tablet PC that offer the same capabilities without the phone service. Currently, mobile technologies have started to permeate into various areas of society, including learning and education where mobile devices are now used both formally and informally. Formally, in that the users are prompted to use mobile devices for learning, and informally, where the users are seeking out their own learning experiences.

Although it appears as if mobile devices have only recently achieved the performance capabilities to be useful as educational and learning tools, the idea of mobile educational and learning technologies was established by Kay Alan in the 1960s [89]. In 1972, Kay expounded the idea of a personal computer for children of all ages, which described a computer device very similar to the contemporary tablet PCs such as the Samsung Tab or Apples iPad. Years after Kays vision, computers have been developed to be more personal and cost efficient. In the early 1990s, huge advances in technology led to the design of wireless devices such as personal digital assistants (PDAs) and phones that can support mobile activities. As mobile devices became more powerful, capable and more manageable in size, the significant decrease in the cost of such devices enabled a large number of users to purchase their own wireless devices. The most popular device is the cell phone, which remains as the most owned and used device today. In 2010, a survey conducted by Pew Research Center in the United States reported that 85% of adults own cell phones, the majority of which are young people. [90]

The survey found that 90% of adults aged between 30 and 49 own cell phones, whereas 96% of adults aged between 18 and 29 own one. [91] reported that mobile devices are even more prevalent amongst higher education students, where approximately 97% of students born since 1980 own mobile devices. The recent developments in mobile phone capabilities have encouraged many more users to use their mobile phones to access the Internet. In fact, most countries now use wireless Internet connection, especially in developing countries where there are generally insufficient wired network infrastructures and many of their population are only able to access the Internet using their mobile devices [92].

4.3. Definitions and Theoretical Background of M-Learning

The fact that mobile devices are capable of various functionalities and come in small sizes means they can be used effectively to support a variety of learning activities. However, the breadth of support makes specifying and developing theories associated with M-learning extremely problematic [93]. In looking for a theory, Traxler claimed that the M-learning community is over simplifying M-learning by focusing just on the importance of E-learning, and he considers the issue of transferability [93]. [43] maintained that M-learning is associated with more than one theory, and examined mobile activity involving collaborative, constructivist and behaviorist categories, as well as coordination, in situated and informal environments. Additional research has shown that social constructivist theory [94] and conversation theory [95] facilitate collaborative learning and individualized communication, and are, therefore, also suited to mobile environments [96, 97, 98]. Navigations [99] and connectives [100] have also been proposed as suitable to mobile environments due to the fact that communities are increasingly learning through practice, work-related tasks and personal networks. Moreover, he theory that activity is implicit as part of a system of cultural historical activity, it is also associated with M-learning [101, 102, 103].

There are two mains areas of focus in the definitions of M-learning; mobile device size and technology and its mobility [93]. Sharples argued that M-learning can be defined by the context it is used in, and the users' experience and their backgrounds [103]. Table 4.1 provides an overview of M-learning different definitions of M-learning. Definitions suggested in the most current literature and research surveys frequently describes M-learning as being knowledge construction across life situations and within different contexts, and being enabled by technology and learner mobility. M-learning is also often considered the next generation of D-learning and an extension of E-learning.

M-learning can be defined as mobile technology based learning and may also be referred to as S-learning or 'smart device' based learning. Ubiquitous learning (U-learning) is similar to some forms of simple M-learning, in that learning environments can be accessed in different situations and contexts.

Table 4.1. An overview of M-learning definitions

Source	Definition
[104]	"E-learning using mobile computational devices: Palms, Windows CE machines, even your digital cell phone."
[105]	An approach to E-learning or just another channel that delivers the same materials
[106]	"Any sort of learning that happens when the learner is not at a fixed, predetermined location or learning that happens when the learner takes advantage of the learning opportunities offered by mobile technologies."
[107]	"Any form of e-learning (studying) and teaching that occurs through a mobile devices, or in a mobile environment."
[5]	"A new stage of e-learning having the ability to learn everywhere at every time through use of mobile and portable devices."
[108]	"The provision of education and training on PDAs/palmtop/handhelds, smartphones and mobile devices."
[99]	A type of E-learning that specifically uses wireless devices for learning support and content delivery.
[56]	"Any educational provision where the sole or dominant technologies are handheld or palmtop devices."
[109]	A next stage or a new form of e-learning through the use of mobile and portable devices and wireless network and communication technology for teaching and learning"
[110]	"The digital support of adaptive, investigative, communicative, collaborative, and productive learning activities in remote locations which offer a variety of contexts for the teacher to operate in"
[111]	"Processes of coming to know through conversations across multiple contexts amongst people and personal interactive technologies."
[50]	A new mechanism of education using mobile devices as learning tools to obtain the required educational information services and resources at anytime and anywhere.
[8]	As a special type of E-learning, bound by different capabilities and characteristics, including different network technology properties.
[112]	Learning using wireless and mobile computing technologies to promote learners nomadicity and mobility nature.
[113]	"The process of using mobile device to access learning materials and to communicate with fellow students, instructors or institution."
[114]	"intersection of mobile computing with elearning, learning enabled by the use of PDAs, mobile phones other personal and portable devices."
[115]	"Rudiments of ubiquitous learning."
[116]	"Fourth wave of learning: using the Internet.
[117]	Learning using ICT in mobile contexts.

4.4. M-Learning Characteristics

This ubiquitous nature, and the ability to personalize learning, is important components of M-learning that distinguish it from other learning methods and environments. [118] summarized M-learning as "flexibility, ubiquity of access to information, and motivating increased engagement, mobile technologies and infrastructure facilitate this revolution of always-on learning, accessible to the masses, but tailored to the individual". [119, 120] both believe that M-learning can provide learning that is just-for-me, just-in-time, just-enough, which means that necessary information, can be learned without having to understand the context of that information. There is a large amount of existing literature on M-learning, which provides a general overview of the following M-learning characteristics:

- **Portable** the weight and small size of mobile devices supports the mobility and portability of the devices to different sites or locations. This M-learning characteristic can effectively support a wide range of learning activities. It supports each individual learner to have a personal interaction with the technology in an authentic and appropriate context of use [43, 121, 122, 123, 124, 125].

- **Simple to use and learn** M-learning does not require extra effort for learners to learn how to use specific M-learning tools and devices. Using personal mobile devices as learning tools is easy for learners, as they are already familiar with all of its functionalities. M-learning opportunities would allow learners to learn and study in different places easily [122, 123, 126, 127].

- **Interactive** M-learning, as an extension of e-learning, is interactive. The learner drives the direction of the learning process rather than sitting passively whilst others, such as an instructor, direct the learning process or provide the required data. M-learning has to be interactive because it relies on data provided by servers and the learner has to employ their judgment in deciding what data to examine [128, 129, 54, 130, 131].

- **Context sensitive** context is a vital characteristic of M-learning, because without context learning, every learner would have the same learning experience. Mobile technologies have extended learning into more stimulating environments than the T-learning approach and support learners to investigate real problems. Mobile technologies also facilitate obtaining required information in context to make connections between personal experience and formal knowledge. In order to capture context information, mobile devices use various kinds of sensors, e.g. bio-sensors, environmental sensors and activity sensors[129, 132, 133, 119, 134, 135, 41, 136].

- **Flexible** the learning process can take place anywhere and at any time. Learning can happen on the move and across different places. M-learning can take advantage of learning opportunities offered by portable or mobile technologies [122, 123, 137, 126, 127].

- **Collaborative** through the use of M-learning, learners can share the same material, which might lead to receiving instant tips and feedback. In this situation, the learning process reduces any communication and cultural barriers between instructors and their learners by using learners preferred communication channels [129, 138, 133, 139, 140, 135].

- **Privacy** M-learning is private, but this does not mean that the knowledge and information learned cannot be discussed or shared with other learners during the learning process, or that data and learning materials are only accessible by individual learners. To be more precise, it means that individual learners can access M-learning contents whenever it suits them, and collect the required data independently from other learners [43, 139, 119, 134, 135].

- **Expediency** the most important advantage of M-learning is its expediency in defining and supporting new learning techniques. Because learners are able to access the Internet anywhere using a mobile device, they are able to integrate technologies to upload images straight from their mobile devices rather than waiting to return to school. Furthermore, learners are able to use mobile devices in shops to check if there is a particular food stuff they need for a home economics lesson[141, 142, 129, 132, 121, 127, 140, 143].

- **Individualistic** modern learners are more confident about using their mobile devices as learning tools, which impacts greatly on their learning process. Moreover, learners have special relationships with their mobile devices, creating an environment that reflects the identity of the owner, their lifestyle and interests. The improvements in mobile technologies in terms of learning has further developed this environment and made it more personal and complete [138, 129, 121, 144, 136].

- **Pervasive** in terms of M-learning, pervasive means that the learner is able to freely perform a learning activity, which might involve co-operating or collaborating with other learners using different types of networks and multiple devices as the learner moves around an environment. Pervasiveness is a crucial M-learning characteristic that emphasizes context-awareness to bridge the gap between the real world and the virtual world, allowing context utilization of real world information and objects in the learning process [138, 145, 146, 147].

- **Accessibility** this is a key factor in the success of any M-learning initiative. Currently, mobile devices provide access to all available learning materials from virtually anywhere and at any time. However, many learning and education providers fail to address the issue of accessibility until after M-learning devices have been purchased, and instructors are often left struggling to find online learning tools to meet the needs of learners with disabilities [121, 125].

The studies mentioned above highlight the fact that M-learning can support and improve students' learning. M-learning is depicted as being portable and able to support access to learning anywhere and anytime. It is simple to use and learn user friendly, and familiar, interactive and encourages engagement. Mobile learning can also enhance the participation of learners. In addition, mobile learning is context sensitive; it supports learning within the students context, situation and locality. Further crucial characteristics are flexibility and accessibility, and its collaborative, pervasive, individualistic and user-centered nature. M-learning supports learner expediency, quick access to information 'just-in-time' and it also facilitates communication. The list of M-learning characteristics merely serves as a simple way to understanding the concept of M-learning.

4.5. M-Learning Methods

Generally speaking, learning is a continuous process that does not stop even after students have left school, and learning experiences do not stop. This is especially true given the high proliferation of mobile devices and technologies that are used for different purposes regarding learning, education and communication. The abundance of mobile devices and technologies creates new learning opportunities, meaning that mobile technologies can play a major role across varied learning environments. This is especially true in terms of informal learning, where mobile technologies can be used to enable collaboration, communication, and information sharing between learners [148]. The classroom is a physical environment where learners study and acquire knowledge, which can be classified as a formal learning method; whereas virtual learning is defined as learning outside a formal learning environment and can be classified as an informal learning method. Therefore, learners are frequently engaged in a learning process that switches between both formal and informal learning methods [149].

M-learning bridges the gap between the formal physical learning environment and the virtual learning space, in other words, between formal and informal learning [145, 140]. Learning is not restricted to a specific place or time and, therefore, formal education cannot offer learners all the required skills and knowledge [150]. Moreover, M-learning is believed to eliminate learning formalities [151], and offer a range of choices of medium for learning [140]. There is a vast body of research concerning the implementation of M-learning activities, most of which supports the idea of the affiliation between the physical learning environment and the outside world, thereby bringing real contexts, e.g. real world issues, into the physical learning space or classroom. Kukulska-Hulme conducted a review of European M-learning projects and concluded that a combination of fixed and mobile technologies can support different learning experiences. The concept of informal and non-formal learning is typically distinct from formal learning [152].

4.5.1. Formal M-Learning

Formal M-learning is purposeful learning that is usually offered by education or training institutions. This type of M-learning typically takes place in learning environments that are specially designed for learning, training and teaching, and usually requires specialist and qualified learning facilitators to teach the subject. Moreover, formal M-learning is intentional, organized and structured in terms of learning objectives, methods, time, and support, and it is often guided by a learning program or other type of formal curriculum. Formal M-learning can be viewed as externally directed learning, because learning progress is monitored, controlled, assessed and verified externally, leading to the awarding of certificates or diplomas to recognize learning achievements.

4.5.2. Non-formal M-Learning

Non-formal M-learning is purposeful learning that is not usually offered by education providers. This type of M-learning takes place in a diverse range of environments that are not specially designed for learning, training and teaching, and where M-learning is not one of their core activities. Non-formal M-learning does not generally lead to certification of the learning achieved. Traditionally, non-formal M-learning is aimed at specific groups, but seldom documents or evaluates the learning achievements and results using conventional, visible techniques. However, similarly to formal M-learning, non-formal M-learning is structured in terms of learning objectives, methods, time, and support. In contrast to formal M-learning, non-formal M-learning is self-directed learning, because learning progress is monitored, controlled, assessed and verified by the learner and is planned from the learners point of view.

4.5.3. Informal M-Learning

Informal M-learning is non-purposeful learning that is not offered by education providers. This type of learning typically takes place in the context of everyday life; at work, in the community and with family. Informal M-learning results from the activities of daily life associated with learning activities. Unlike formal and non-formal M-learning, informal M-learning is not structured in terms of learning objectives, methods, time, and support and normally does not lead to certification of the learning. Moreover, informal M-learning is never organized, and rather than being directed by an inflexible curriculum, it is usually contemplated spontaneously and experientially. Evidently, informal M-learning does lead to results and achievements, but these are virtually never certified and rarely recorded.

The key distinction between these concepts of M-learning methods is that both formal and non-formal M-learning methods provide structured learning in terms of learning objectives, methods and time, whereas informal M-learning does not. The other key difference is that formal and non-formal M-learning methods are intentional, whilst informal M-learning is usually a non-intentional learning activity. In addition there are contextual differences between the three methods, as both informal and non-formal M-learning are self-directed activities, whereas formal M-learning is externally directed towards the learning objectives [153, 154, 155].

4.6. M-Learning Components

There are four main components that need to be considered in dealing with M-learning systems:

- Stakeholders.
- Mobile device.
- Mobile app.
- Learning material.

4.6.1. Stakeholders

M-learning stakeholders include the learners, the instructor, the administrator and the developer. The instructor is responsible for providing the learning material and also for providing accurate and timely learning information required by the learners. The administrator is responsible for the general administration and co-ordination of all related aspects of learning using mobile devices, including updating learning activities, maintaining learning content and evaluation of learning solutions. The developer is responsible for developing and maintaining stakeholders' requirements. The learner is an M-learning user who is learning about a particular topic. Learning style has been defined as an individual's approach and characteristics for processing and organizing information [156]. Every learner has their own individual learning method or style, and the learner needs to understand the learning process and to understand these styles or mechanisms. Typically, the structure of learning consists of two steps; information reception and processing. In the first step, internal information becomes available to the learners. The availability of learning material is a very important component in the second step, as the learner selects and utilizes learning materials. The various learning styles need to be analyzed in order to determine the preferences of those who need to be supported so that they can be catered for [157]. The ways in which learners study varies considerably. There are those who learn best using different reading techniques, e.g. skimming or scanning, whilst others learn by using the sequential learning technique of going through the whole material. Clearly, the learning material provided by M-learning will definitely satisfy all of these learning techniques. Moreover, M-learning also supports visual learning by enabling learners to see visualizations of learning material, e.g. building a bridge or tower.

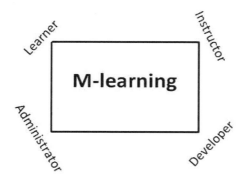

Figure 4.1. An Overview of M-learning Stakeholders.

Most M-learning applications present information visually as diagrams, pictures and tables. Since many learners prefer this kind of information, it would be easy for them to use an M-learning application that enhances the usability of their M-learning device. M-learning also supports accessibility, as text-to-speech on mobile devices makes the learning process easier for learners with disabilities. A further benefit of M-learning is that it enables the learner to review the learning material at anytime and anywhere. M-learning enables learners to communicate and interact with other learners, for instance through VOIP or discussion boards. Learners can also utilize mobile devices to receive specific information about any preferred subject during studying [158].

4.6.2. Mobile Device

In recent years, mobile devices have become multifunctional tools capable of providing a wide range of applications connected to everyday activities. The term 'mobile device' can be used to refer to a wide range of consumer electronics. Typically, mobile device refers to any hardware device that has the ability to connect to the Internet. Mobile device categories include:

- Tablet PC is classified as a type of notebook computer device with an LCD screen offering the capability to write on it using a stylus. The handwriting can be converted into digital standard text using device handwriting recognition, or saved as handwritten text. There are different types of Table PCs such as IBM Thinkpad, Fujitsu Lifebook, Toshiba Portege, Samsung Q1, and Motion Computing.

- Personal Digital Assistant (PDA) or pocket computers are handheld devices that combine many components of computing ability, Internet access, network connection and telephone calls in single device. The different types of PDA devices include the Compaq iPaq, Sony Clie, Palm Pilot, Toshiba Pocket PC, Casio Cassiopedia, Hewlett-Packard Jornado and Revo.

- Smartphones have the capability of both handheld computers and mobile phones in a single device. Smartphones supports program installation and information storing, along with the use of a mobile phone for calling or messaging. There are different types of Smartphones, including Blackberry, Nokia T-Mobile Sidekick, Palm Treo, Sony Ericsson, Motorola Q, E-Ten, I-mate, HP iPaq, Torq.

Generally, mobile devices have different capabilities, e.g. voice and phone communications, text messaging (using SMS short message service or MMS multimedia message service), short-range communication (using RFID radio frequency identification, Bluetooth or NFC near field communication), camera capturing (images, videos and QR quick response code reading), internal sensors (accelerometer, proximity, compass, gyroscope and barometer), Geolocation (including maps , GPS globe position system and geo-fencing), playback or media viewer (using audio, video, image and podcast), Microphone involving podcast and voice recording, notification (sound, alert, and vibrate), search facility (search engine, discovery, quick-reference), document viewer (eBook and PDF) and touchscreen interaction capability [53]. Mobile devices with these capabilities are usually seen as an extension to normal desktop devices. However, most of these devices have common limitations such as limited input capabilities with small keys and, even the devices with keyboards, they are still small which is inconvenient for extensive use. However M-learning approaches tend to be click-centered not type-centered approaches, similar to E-learning. The screens in mobile devices are generally too small to be used in any complex applications. Additionally, their memory capacity is too small and the applications run on mobile devices need to be battery-friendly for lower power consumption [65].

4.6.3. Mobile App

Mobile apps are just as important a component of M-learning as the learners and mobile devices. Mobile apps are one of the main cornerstones of M-learning environments, and robust mobile apps are necessary to deliver learning materials in an efficient manner to meet learners' objectives. Currently, there are a wide range of mobile devices available in the market, starting from a low end handset device to the Samsung Galaxy and iPhone devices with beautifully designed touch screen interfaces. These devices are capable of hosting a wide range of different applications. These mobile apps can be provided pre-installed by the manufacturer on the mobile device or as downloaded apps via web apps obtained over HTTP or through different mobile apps distribution platforms [157]. M-learning apps can be found as documentary applications that might include PDF, PPT, DOC, etc, as website apps that involve either static websites that may consist of HTML and CSS formats or interactive sites that may consist of JavaScript functionalities. In addition, stand-alone apps can be developed using programming languages, such as C++, C#, Java etc [158]. Mobile apps are classified into three types based on the application building architecture:

Native App

The implementation and deployment of native apps are dependent on using a hardware device with a mobile device hardware abstraction layer that makes all the hardware features available for use, e.g. audio, graphics, camera and network connectivity. Native apps have binary executable files that can be downloaded directly and stored locally in the mobile device. There are several places to download native apps, including Androids Marketplace, Apples App Store, or BlackBerrys App World and other mobile vendors. Native app development has the following advantages:

- Ability to access different device features, e.g. media, communication, location and graphics capabilities.

- Performance; native apps are able to interact directly with the underlying system APIs so that the native app's performance is high in terms of reliability and speed.

- Security; the native app supports the use of the device's available security features, such as the facility to lock the device. Therefore, storing data in a mobile device is much safer than storing it on a web application [65, 159].

Web App

The term mobile web app refers to Internet enabled applications that have particular mobile device functionalities. They are accessed via the web browser of mobile devices, such as Safari on Apple products, and they do not require anything else to be downloaded and installed onto the device in advance. Web browsers are common mobile app technology that is available on the majority of modern mobile devices, such as Smartphones, PDAs and Tablet PCs. These have powerful browsers that support different web technologies, including Sheets 3 (CSS3), Cascading Style, HTML5 capabilities and advanced JavaScript. HTML5 web apps became very popular because they support the same level of functionality as native apps in the browser. Web app browsers are usually built on different mobile app frameworks, but they generally use the mobile service providers network for internet connection, or connect through a wireless local area network, using HTTP over TCP/IP for displaying web pages that are written in HTML, XHTML MP or WML. Thus, the developers of mobile apps are looking to the web browser technology to resolve any issues whenever possible. There are two main approaches to web apps: mobile browsing and mobile-optimized websites. Both approaches have been designed to provide comfortable touch technology on small screen sizes. Moreover, some companies redesigned the look of their mobile website to be similar to a native app that can be launched using shortcuts. Mobile apps are available via two different models of web browser:

- AJAX is a synchronous JavaScript and XML model based upon Rich Internet Application (RIA) that is implemented in mobile applications.

- Widget means a downloadable mobile app that looks and acts similar to traditional desktop PC applications, and these apps are developed using web browser technologies including HTML, CSS and JavaScript.

One of the most noticeable advantages of the mobile web app is that it is inexpensive to develop something that supports multiplatforms. In addition, the development of mobile web apps does not require any type of software development kits (SDKs) [160, 161, 65, 159].

Hybrid App

Hybrid mobile apps are similar to native apps as they are written using web technologies (HTML5, JavaScript and CSS) and run on mobile devices. Hybrid apps run inside a native container. A web-to-native abstraction layer allows access to device capabilities that are not accessible in mobile web apps, such as the local storage, camera and accelerometer. Generally, hybrid mobile apps are run or hosted inside the mobile device's native container and are written using the same technologies that are used to build websites and mobile web apps. Thus, it can be viewed as a marriage between web technology and native execution. One of the most noticeable advantages of the hybrid app is its cross-platform development. Due to the reusability of the same components of HTML code on different mobile operating systems, the cost of development is significantly reduced. Tools such as Sencha Touch and PhoneGap allow developers to design and implement code across platforms, with the use of HTML [159].

4.6.4. Learning Material

Learning materials are the information delivered to learners as the result of searches to obtain the required knowledge [162]. The learner's required knowledge might be obtained by scanning, surveying or reading the learning contents or materials. In order to keep learners interested in gaining knowledge, the learning materials should be current and new to them. Naturally, there is a strong relationship between learning styles, mobile device capabilities, mobile apps and learning materials. Therefore, any mismatch between these four components will lead to a lack of motivation in utilizing M-learning. In turn, that might lead to usability issues, e.g. lack of ability to understand and learn [163]. M-learning material should be prepared in various formats, with different versions offering the learner the right to choose their preferred learning materials. Mobile devices use different functionalities and capabilities, which forces M-learning developers to structure learning materials in such a way as to be compatible with different types of mobile devices, especially as learners do not all prefer to use the same types of devices. M-learning developers can use XML extensible markup language (XML) to offer learners the same learning materials that work across different platforms. In such cases, the learning materials can be transferred dynamically to a variety of mobile devices [139]. In fact, it is very important for M-learning developers to understand the various learning styles and develop robust M-learning apps to not only provide learning materials in different formats and to run on different devices, but to also be compatible with a variety of learning styles. This will ensure that M-learning apps and devices reach the desirable level of quality to help different types of learners receives higher levels of knowledge [158]. There are many learning materials in the form of images and multimedia that are not normally supported by mobile devices. The learning material handled by the M-learning apps needs to be structured into smaller units, in order to be readable and displayable in small screens. Furthermore, connectivity could be problematic, so there should be support for offline learning, enabling learners to download learning materials onto their device [65].

4.7. Summary

The objective of this chapter was to discuss the various M-learning definitions and the theoretical background, and to provide an overview of M-learning characteristics and methods, as well as explaining the components of M-learning. The objective has been achieved as an overview of M-learning history was provided in section 4.2 and the different M-learning definitions and theoretical background were discussed in section 4.3. A general overview of M-learning characteristics and methods, including formal, non-formal and informal M-learning methods, was provided in sections 4.4 and 4.5 respectively. Finally, the four main M-learning components of learner, mobile device, learning material and mobile app were explained in section 4.6.

Chapter 5

M-Learning Requirements

Objectives

- Provide an overview of M-learning tools.
- Discuss M-learning pedagogical, social and cultural requirements.
- Discuss M-learning business, economic and technical requirements.

5.1. Introduction

This chapter provides an overview of M-learning Tools. It discusses different M-learning requirements and is divided into five sections. Section 5.2 introduces the M-learning tools. Section 5.3 introduces four different requirements of M-learning applications. 5.4 discusses pedagogical and educational M-learning requirements, as well as detailing its different characteristics, including learning theories, instructional design models, learning material quality, learning material completeness, learning material presentation, learning material organization and learner support options. Section 5.4.1 discusses social and cultural M-learning requirements; such as interaction, acceptability, visibility, sociability, attitude and intellectual property. Section 5.4.2 discusses different business and economic M-learning requirements, including cost, feasibility and cost-effectiveness. Finally 5.4.3 discusses various technical and quality requirements, including availability, response speed, flexibility, scalability and security. Security covers different important characteristics, such as completeness of security, data integrity, privacy, confidentiality and information flow control.

5.2. Overview of M-Learning Tools

Mobility is a primary characteristic of M-learning tools, enabling learners to access technologies, while moving between locations, even across different time zones, using mobile devices (e.g. Tablet, PDA, Smart phone, and wireless laptop). The current mobile computing platforms, with their fast and accessible internet access support many and education and learning usages, e.g. short messaging services, using Bilingual dictionaries for the purpose of language learning, practice questions and vocabulary translation[8, 9]. The fast and easy internet accesses afforded by mobile technologies have prompted M-learning to evolve. However, achieving maximum benefit from M-learning is impossible without access to portable or mobile devices equipped with wireless technology. In addition, the sizes, prices, performance and capabilities of wireless, portable and mobile devices are very significant factors. In addition, availability and ease with which wireless connectivity can be achieved are common M-learning. The most popular devices are those used in the learning or education process and include [164]:

- Normal cellular phones or voice communication devices with access to Internet WAP or GPRS technologies.

- Personal Digital Assistant (PDA). A small size portable device with significant processor power. These use software applications to recognize learners' handwritten text.

- Smart Phones are mobile devices with functionalities similar to cellular phones and PDAs. They have a smaller screen size than a PDA, but one that is bigger than that of a normal cellular phone.

- Tablet PCs are mobile devices with functionalities and performance similar to normal PCs. They can be used without keyboards.

- Notebook computers, have performance and functionalities similar to normal desktop computers, but with a smaller screen. They are able to establish wireless communication but are often expensive.

5.3. M-Learning Requirements

M-learning applications are mobile applications that focus on offering learning activities can take advantage of network wireless technologies and mobility within learning and education processes [128]. The speed of today's Internet technology has improved learners options for interactivity throughout the learning system. The internet enables a high level of interaction between instructors and learners over a distributed geographical area. The Internet supports the creation of learning environments that meet learning systems' objectives and requirements, supporting learners participation in different learning activities, such as, for interaction, discussion, and collaboration for the purpose of problem solving.

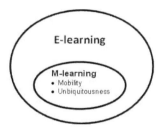

Figure 5.1. M-learning as a subset of E-learning.

The use of Internet technologies has enabled distance learning and E-learning to take place. M-learning is a subset of E-learning that refers to the creation and consumption of learning content and activities by instructors or learners using mobile devices. Authors have defined M-learning as E-learning via a mobile device [165].The primary advantage of the M-learning approach is the ability of accessing to access knowledge anywhere at any time. However, the main concerns and issues associated with M-learning, as the next generation of learning technology, is their ability to combine contemporary and innovative technologies. In addition, there is a drive to provide an innovative learning environment that will be interactive, accessible, flexible and available to all.

The exponential growth in development and research into M-learning applications is a consequence of the flexibility, availability and freedom associated with traditional learning or class based restrictions. Despite their prevalence, and the vast body of work associated with the different learning approaches available, only limited exploration of different learners' and instructors' M-learning requirements has been undertaken. All modern portable and handheld devices support diverse mobile application development, enabling them to provide a large quantity of context aware content to learners and instructors, because the majority of mobile devices are equipped with computational processing power that is similar to that of desktop computers. Mobile applications for learning activities offer diverse benefits and bring complex challenges to mobile applications developers, which are not found or resolved by traditional software engineering applications [166, 167, 168].

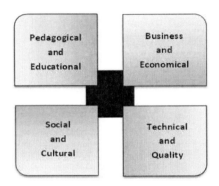

Figure 5.2. M-learning Requirements Dimensions.

The next sections list and discuss general requirements for better M-learning services in accordance with four dimensions:

- Pedagogical and Educational.
- Social and Cultural.
- Business and Economic.
- Technical and Quality.

The requirements for these dimensions are tailored to criteria established from a study of the literature; they offer a standard for software quality, guidelines, personal experience regarding developing and evaluating e-learning applications, evaluation of human-computer interaction, e-commerce, and M-learning applications. The next, sections analyze the requirements each of these four dimensions.

5.4. Pedagogical and Educational

Pedagogical and educational M-learning requirements can be categorized into different areas:

- Learning theories
- Instructional design models
- Learning material quality
- Learning material completeness
- Learning material presentation
- Learning material organization
- Learner Support

Different learning and educational theories, such as cognitivism, behaviorism, constructivism and social learning should be incorporated into the different M-learning applications. In the case of instructional design models, different instructional design models such as analysis, design, implementation, test, evaluation and maintenance should be included in the M-learning applications. Learning material quality must be valid and trustworthy. Learning materials should be both appropriate and useful, to achieve target educational objectives. The learning materials should be designed to effectively motivate learners. In terms of completeness of learning materials, the learning material should be comprehensive enough to cover all the main ideas, topics and key points at the appropriate level and in an ideal quantity, considering M-learning restrictions associated with screen size, memory, input...etc.

The presentation of learning materials should be based on a variety of high quality media, such as normal text, graphs, images, pictures, chart, diagrams, audio and video. The learning materials should be organized so that they are modular, flexible and simple. They should also be organized to be easily navigated using various navigation tools; i.e. directories, tables and maps. The learning material structure should be appropriate and acceptable for learners and support educational activities. M-learning applications should support both learners and instructors, as well as reacting to their actions by responding as

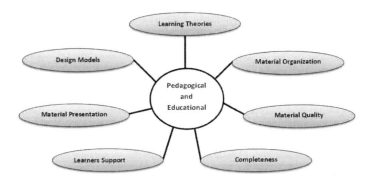

Figure 5.3. Pedagogical and Educational Requirements.

required in the right quantity at the right moment. Finally, M-learning applications should always attract learner's attention, challenging, stimulating, provoking, encouraging and building the confidence of the learner. In addition, it should provide different support facilities; i.e. collaboration, communication, sharing, searching or navigation, help, dictionary, glossary, FAQ, references, bibliography, and documentation [169].

5.4.1. Social and Cultural

Social and cultural requirements can be categorized according to different areas:

- Interaction
- Acceptability
- Visibility
- Sociability
- Attitude
- Intellectual Property

M-learning applications should support different social communication and interaction styles and modes; i.e. visual or oral, formal or informal. Social interaction and communication should be flexible and support multilingualism, e.g. use of translators or interpreters.

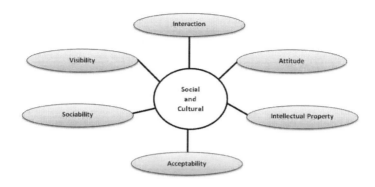

Figure 5.4. Social and Cultural Requirements.

M-learning application should be acceptable to, and supportive of, various cultural, social, religious and political values and ideas. It should not include elements that discriminate either by race, age group, gender or health. M-learning applications should be visible and observable, and there should be no concealed activities integrated into them. All information, activities, applications and decisions should be available and visible, according to the learners requests, e.g. the learners transactions should not be recorded or monitored from a security perspective. M-learning applications should support and promote the learner in the areas of socialization, friendship, sharing, cooperation, relationship development, mutual understanding, active participation and responsibility.

M-learning applications should encourage learners to be confident and committed, by supporting self-efficacy, self-esteem and the opportunity to learn more and gain knowledge. Regarding intellectual property, learner should always be able to trust that no one will access his/her data, achievements, records, activities, reports, and results ... etc. without his/her authorization and approval. The intellectual property of learners should also be assured [169].

5.4.2. Business and Economic

Business and economic M-learning requirements can be categorized into different areas:

- Cost
- Feasibility

- Cost-Effectiveness

Cost should be kept low throughout the entire lifetime of the M-learning application. The costs, including development, operations, upgrades, maintenance or replace should be kept low.

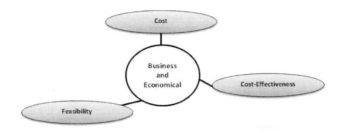

Figure 5.5. Business and Economic Requirements.

The M-learning application should be economically feasible for implementation and operation. There are also potential health issues, such as addiction or eye problems, and environmental issues and risks that also need to be considered. M-learning applications should always achieve the maximum benefits and target results at the lowest conceivable costs, compared with other mobile applications that have the same results intended.

5.4.3. Technical and Quality

M-learning requirements can be categorized according to their different characteristics: [169, 170]:

- Availability
- Quick Response
- Flexibility
- Scalability
- Connectivity
- Performance

M-Learning Requirements

Figure 5.6. Technical and Software Quality Characteristics.

- Reliability
- Functionality
- Usability
- Efficiency
- Maintainability
- User Interface
- Security

This chapter considers thirteen technical and software quality characteristics.

5.4.4. Availability

The availability of M-learning applications relates the time ratio for the use of the application, while the software component is functional, to the expected or required total time associated with the function of the M-learning application. Learners always require the maximum level of availability that can be provided through different services or M-learning applications [167]. The high availability of M-learning applications is a key feature of software products that users and companies depend on today. Mobile applications in general, and M-learning applications in particular are essential to learners' applications, i.e. bilingual mobile dictionary, email software tools, mobile discussion ports and mobile banking programs. Moreover, there are different M-learning applications within the data center, which support learning with high availability, as effective learning tools, such as, students mobile discussion ports with Voice over Internet Protocol (VoIP) and audio and video file sharing application capabilities. However, M-learning applications might suffer from low service quality or impair the availability of different mobile applications [171].

5.4.5. Quick Response

Services provided through M-learning applications must make serious provisions to respond quickly and efficiently to outages, and ensure the continuity of M-learning services. One of the important factors that need to be considered when providing different M-learning application services is the ability to recover from outages seamlessly and efficiently. Many factors lead to the quick response failure of M-learning applications, such as power and processor failures, configuration errors, network hardware faults, server hardware faults, connectivity failure, M-learning application bugs, compatibility and other performance concerns. M-learning applications should be designed to quickly respond to and minimize downtime for both planned and unplanned requests and service interruptions. This helps ensure learners have continuous access to various M-learning applications, such as, instant messaging, e-mail, and other critical applications and data, to perform tasks effectively.

5.4.6. Flexibility

Flexibility and ease of use are crucial characteristics of M-learning applications, which might be defined in a number of different ways. Different learners might employ different definitions and meaning depending on their area of concern. M-learning applications are ranked according to their simplicity of use, for both the instructors and learners. Thus, ease of use and flexibility are not product items, but process issues and concerns. Therefore, M-learning application developers should be able to offer learners flexible services and plans to allow an enterprise to quickly and efficiently adopt changes. Moreover, M-learning developers should also aim to support accessibility of information any time and any place. An M-learning application that is perceived as easy and flexible enough to use is an unacceptable option if the output does not meet the instructors' and learners' needs. Ease of use and flexibility are top priorities for M-learning applications. Therefore, M-learning applications consider greater functionality with the flexibility and ease of use capabilities at the design stage.

5.4.7. Scalability

Scalability is very important as distinguishing factors of M-learning applications. Elasticity or scalability of M-learning application means that resource allocation can become smaller or bigger in response to demand. In a condition of rapid elasticity, consumers can increase or decrease capacity in response to demand. Scalability in the context of M-learning refers to the ability of an M-learning application to scale when adding users or when changing the requirements of the application itself. Elasticity and scalability allow the environment to automatically and ideally assign a dynamic number of resources to a service. Using horizontal scalability can accommodate multiple M-learning users accessing the same learning services, and hosting multiple tenants on the same resource. However, vertical scalability is used only for storage, which grows with the user requirements but cannot be used for parallelized applications.

5.4.8. Connectivity

The connectivity of M-learning application should adhere to open architectures and should comply with different international standards. The connectivity of M-learning applications should also be easy and compatible, allowing them to work with other devices, databases, networks, data formats and platforms. M-learning applications should support a variety of connectivity, different devices, operating systems, communication protocol, data formats and browsers. In terms of portability, M-learning applications should make it easy to export and import from other systems services and data. Moreover, M-learning application modules need to be easily reused by other systems. It should be possible to easily increase number of supported learners, mobility patterns, services and data. M-learning applications should require extra hardware and software but minimum resources to operate.

5.4.9. Performance

One of the main criteria of an M-learning application's performance is the application's energy consumption. The application should not consume a lot of energy. The communication bandwidth of an M-learning application should adjust its operation to the available bandwidth in case of lack of availability of bandwidth. The M-learning application should also use appropriate memory management techniques to increase performance. The M-learning application should also utilize the available input and output devices to the greatest possible extent. The M-learning application should provide quality for the transmitted audio packets and also enhance the quality of the displayed images, so they are the best possible for the available screen size and resolution.

5.4.10. Reliability

M-learning applications should be available in any environment, and quick and easy to install on any appropriate system or device. It should be possible to reconfigure M-learning applications without any difficulties, and parts should be replaceable, in case of a need for modification in operation and scope. In addition, M-learning applications should be fast and easy to revise and upgrade. They should also be error free applications, allowing all operations to be consistent, correct, accurate and error free (faults).

5.4.11. Functionality

The M-learning application functionality should be suitable and useful to meet various educational and learning objectives, learner, instructors and the situation. M-learning applications should be simple, flexible, convenient and self-explanatory, to offer service provision to suit demand. The M-learning application should offer different communication modes, such as synchronous or asynchronous, user to user, or user to device etc. M-learning applications should support mobility anywhere, across bigger coverage areas, at any mobility processing speed. M-learning applications should support the running of multiple functions concurrently with no interference between operations.

5.4.12. Usability

M-learning applications should be accessible and usable by as many users as possible, regardless of ability, age and state or condition. In addition, they should support different languages and types of communication, including learners with special needs. M-learning applications should provide different tools and formats for learner support. The protocols for M-learning application use should be easy to learn, remember, understand, and use. Finally, M-learning applications should attract learners' attention and focus.

5.4.13. Efficiency

The efficiency of M-learning applications is critical. They should have the capacity to respond to changes very quickly and in an appropriate manner; e.g. M-learning systems detect that learners access a specific area, and then the system responds by transmitting a message to the learners immediately. The main concern arising with M-learning applications is the possibility that they might impact on efficiency. Learners should not notice any delays in response to their requests and communications. The time processing, communicating and storing data should be less than the threshold for efficient M-learning application deployment.

5.4.14. Maintainability

The ease of maintenance of M-learning applications is very important. They should be designed so that minimum time and effort is required to maintain efficient operations. M-learning applications should be able to recognize and prevent errors when continuously monitoring state. Any faults that cannot be prevented should be fixed easily with limited resources, time and effort. Moreover, there should not be any data or other resources lost in response to errors. Applications should not be stacked creating a deadlock.

5.4.15. User Interface

User interface layout and organization should be intuitive and simple, and the design should be attractive, aesthetically appealing and fun to use. The M-learning applications user interface should support various high quality media types, such as text, audio and video. It should also be easy, simple and intuitive to navigate. The M-learning application should offer appropriate, useful and meaningful methods, by which to improve user productivity. Moreover, M-learning applications should predict actions and changes, and be tailored to the individual user in response to modification that is transparent to learners, immediate and effective.

5.4.16. Security

The main security properties (availability, integrity and confidentiality) are becoming very important aspects in the design of secure M-learning applications. These properties are necessary to secure M-learning application components; such as data, software and hardware resources. The M-learning requirements for security can be categorized into:

- Security Completeness
- Data Integrity
- Privacy and Confidentiality
- Information Flow Control

Figure 5.7 describes the categories of M-learning requirements for Security:

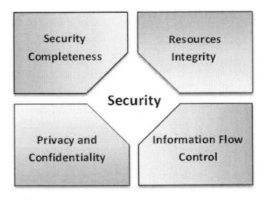

Figure 5.7. of M-learning Requirements for Security.

Security Completeness

The security completeness of an M-learning application should incorporate newly and updated security technologies, such as different access control models, authorization, authentication, certification, firewalls, anti-virus, tunneling, encryption, cryptography, anti-spam and anti-spyware. These security technologies should completely protect accessibility, storage and communication of data, M-learning application and hardware resources. The Security of the M-learning application should support multiple levels of security for different learners and resources. The M-learning application should also ensure that legitimate learners and instructors can perform what they are allowed to, or have the right to do. [172].

Integrity

Integrity refers to the resources (data, software and hardware), ensuring that can only be modified by authorized parties or in authorized ways. M-learning data integrity can be defined as the protection of data from unauthorized manipulation; such as, deletion, modification or fabrication, and also ensuring that data and services are not abused, destroyed or stolen. The security of M-learning applications services depends heavily on the security of M-learning application interfaces, as an unauthorized user (learner or instructor) gaining control of them may then alter, delete or fabricate user data. Hardware (network) integrity is another issue that needs to be considered by the M-learning application developers. Due to a wide range of security needs and the high computation and communication costs of applying strong security measures, the M-learning application developers should consider the security requirements requested in detail [173, 174]

Privacy and Confidentiality

One of the main security properties is confidentiality. Only authorized parties or applications should have the ability to access and manipulate protected data, work and results. M-learning application confidentiality refers to the trustworthiness of specific processes or applications that are able to maintain and handle learners' private and personal data securely. M-learning applications interacting with the learners' data must be certified so that they are guaranteed not to introduce additional privacy and confidentiality risks. M-learning developers are responsible for providing secure M-learning applications. They should ensure instructors and learners' privacy. Privacy is a personal requirement, to control the disclosure and propagation of personal information. In addition, it should also be able to conceal user identity. The confidentiality of the data manipulated by M-learning applications is correlated with instructors or learners' authentication. Protecting learners accounts from theft or damage is an instance of a larger issue of controlling access to objects, including memory, devices, software...etc. [175, 176].

Information Flow Control

An information flow control for M-learning applications can be defined according to the prevention of sensitive information leaking out of its path. Information flow control aims to fill the gaps left by standard security technologies. Information flow occurs from source to target objects whenever information is read from a source that is potentially propagated by the target object. Security in the context of information flow in the M-learning context has three components:

- Information flow requirements, defines how the information should flow from the source to the destination using the M-learning application

- Information flow policy, defines the meaning of secure information flow and establishes what steps should be taken to detect and prevent leakage.

- Information flow mechanisms, enforces information flow policy and focuses on what tools and methods should be used to ensure information flow control.

Using the above mentioned information flow components the user will have control over the data, M-learning application and resources. Generally, Information flow is not a barrier but must be taken into consideration as one of the more important M-learning application design concerns [177].

5.5. Summary

This chapter presented has provided an overview of M-learning applications. It has discussed different M-learning requirements and provided an introduction to four different requirements of M-learning applications. It has discussed pedagogical and educational M-learning requirements and their different characteristics, including learning theories, instructional design models, learning material quality, learning material completeness, learning material presentation, learning material organization and learner support. The chapter also discussed social and cultural M-learning requirements including interaction, acceptability, visibility, sociability, attitude and intellectual property. It also highlighted different business and economic M-learning requirements including cost, feasibility and cost-effectiveness. Finally, it has discussed various technical and Quality requirements including availability, quick response, flexibility, scalability and security. The security requirements covered different important characteristics, such as security completeness, data integrity, privacy, confidentiality and information flow control.

Chapter 6

Frameworks

Objectives

- Give an overview of existing M-learning Frameworks.
- Provide an introduction to different M-learning framework's components.
- Discuss the development and adoption aspects of M-learning frameworks.

6.1. Introduction

This chapter provides an overview of existing M-learning frameworks, and introduces different M-learning framework's components. It discusses the development and adoption aspects associated with different M-learning frameworks, including: the conversational framework for the effective use of learning technologies; the framework for M-learning system based on education components; the design requirements framework for M-learning environments; M-learning: a framework and evaluation, model for framing M-learning; MOTEL: M-learning framework for Geo-Tagging and explorations of sites for learning; M-learning framework for an analog electronics course; MLCF: the M-learning curriculum framework, a hierarchical framework for evaluating the success factors of M-learning; a pedagogical framework for M-learning: categorizing educational applications of mobile technologies into four types; Opencast M-learning framework for enhancing learning in higher education; an ADL M-learning framework, Mobile Learning: Not Just Another Delivery Method and conceptual framework for context-aware M-learning.

6.2. An Overview of M-Learning Frameworks

In order to transition from M-learning academic theorizing to operational, practical and successful use and adoption, M-learning frameworks are necessary. These frameworks are built in order to support different educational providers to implement M-learning in existing or future education curricula.

Table 6.1. An overview of M-learning frameworks

Source	Framework
[178]	Conversational Framework for the Effective Use of Learning Technologies
[179]	Framework for Mobile Learning System Based On Education Component
[180]	A Design Requirements Framework for Mobile Learning Environments
[181]	Mobile learning: A Framework and Evaluation
[182]	A Model for Framing Mobile Learning
[183]	MOTEL: A Mobile Learning Framework for Geo-Tagging and Explorations of Sites for Learning
[184]	Mobile Learning Framework for an Analog Electronics Course
[185]	MLCF: The Mobile Learning Curriculum Framework
[186]	Hierarchical Framework for Evaluating Success Factors of M-learning
[187]	A Pedagogical Framework for Mobile Learning: Categorizing Educational Applications of Mobile Technologies into Four Types
[188]	An Opencast Mobile learning Framework for Enhancing Learning in Higher Education
[189]	ADL Mobile Learning Framework, Mobile Learning: Not Just Another Delivery Method
[41]	Conceptual Framework for Context-aware Mobile Learning

There are a variety of M-learning frameworks. Moreover, many research studies have utilized activity theory, as theoretically for an M-learning framework. [190, 111, 191, 192, 193]

6.3. Existing Approaches of M-Learning Frameworks

Laurillard designed a conversational framework for effective use of learning technologies [178]. Her conversational framework described the irreducible minimum for academic learning. The interplay between theory and practice, which makes the abstract concrete via a reflective practicum, is necessary as is the iterative and continuous dialogue between students and teachers. Figure 6.1 shows Laurillard's conversational framework.

Conversational Framework

Teacher's conception
1. Theory, ideas
2. Conceptions
3. Re-description
4. Re-description
Student's conception

5. Adaptation of task goal in light of student's description
12. Reflection on learners' actions to modify descriptions
10. Adaptation of actions in light of theory, goal, and feedback
11. Reflection on concept in light of experience

Teacher's constructed environment
6. Teacher sets goal
7. Student's action
8. Feedback
9. Student's modified action
Student's actions

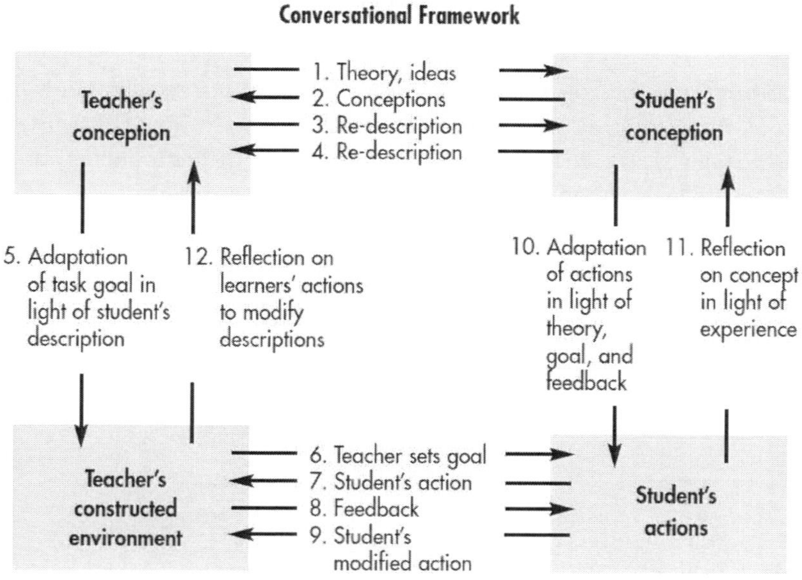

Figure 6.1. Laurillard's conversational framework.

Mostakhdemin has designed a framework for M-learning systems based on educational components [179].

The framework provided focused on M-learning system development and is based on three mobile domains, including usability, E-learning system and wireless technology, as shown in Figure 6.2. Mobile usability refers to validating the services for each mobile device involved in the mobile learning system. An E-learning system includes the needs of V-learning and E-learning components and systems. Wireless technology refers to wireless network infrastructures, ca-

Figure 6.2. Ali's Framework of Mobile Learning Systems.

pabilities and the cost of services. Parsons proposed conceptual framework for M-learning applications provides systematic support for M-learning experience and design [180]. It is based on a combination of game metaphor and several studies of M-learning contexts.

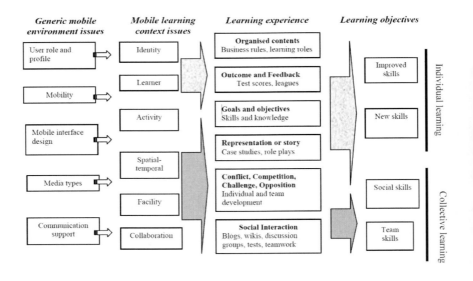

Figure 6.3. M-learning Design Requirements Framework.

It employs accounts of four M-learning projects to explore the relationship between the framework and M-learning design requirements in practice. The design requirements framework for M-Learning environments provides forward engineering support for the successful design of future M-learning systems. Figure 6.3 shows Laurillard's conversational framework.

Motiwalla designed an application framework for M-learning [181]. His framework consists of two levels of research and analysis. The first level is mobile connectivity, which focuses on the applications and technology used by commercial establishments for extending E-commerce.

	Personalized Content	Collaborative Content	
PUSH Mechanism	*Pedagogical Agents & Mentors*	*Communication Aids*	*SMS, IM, Alerts, Scheduling Calendars*
PULL Mechanism	*System Tools & Resources*	*Simulated Classrooms*	*WML websites, Discussion Boards & Chat Forums*
	Alerts, Scheduling Calendars, WML websites	*SMS, IM, Discussion Boards & Chat Forums*	⇐ M-learning Applications

Figure 6.4. M-learning Framework.

The second level is E-learning, which focuses on the Internet and other Information used, and Communication Technology in education. The framework designed, as shown in Figure 6.4 integrates ideas from E-learning and mobile connectivity into application requirements for M-learning. [182] provided a model for framing M-learning that describes M-learning as a process resulting from the convergence of human learning capacities, mobile technologies and social interactions. The framework addresses contemporary pedagogical issues associated with information overload, knowledge navigation and collaboration in learning. This model is useful for guiding the development of future mobile devices, the development of learning materials and the design of teaching and learning strategies for use in mobile education.

The three circles in Figure 6.5 represent the learner, the device and social aspects. The intersections, where the two circles overlap, contain attributes that belong to both aspects. The intersections labeled as interactive learning contain instructional and learning theories, with an emphasis on social constructivism.

The attributes of social technology and device usability intersections de-

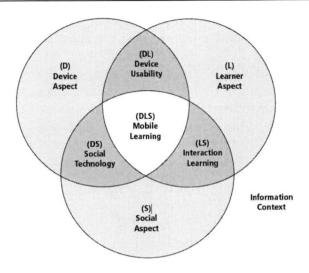

Figure 6.5. The FRAME Model.

scribe the mobile technology affordances [194]. All three aspects overlap at the primary intersection; M-learning in the center.

Baggetun designed an M-learning framework for Geo-Tagging and for the exploration of sites for learning known as MOTEL [183]. The framework comprises an open source Java ME application for mobile telephones, GPS and the server back end for receiving, storing and publishing notes. The application allows the user to create notes and tables easily. The notes are easily edited and stored locally on the phone or sent to the central server database, which can be retrieved later in the field. The MOTEL framework is shown in Figure 6.6.

Madeira proposed using an M-learning Framework for an analog electronics course [184], Figure 6.7.

Their framework was designed as a typical client/server architecture, with two tier separation. The clients followed e-learning as a web tool module, which was made available through a web browser. An offline module, in the form of an iDVD interactive DVD or E-book, which can be carried easily by students and is an M-learning tool, with a competitive module and a reduced version of the e-learning content.

Botha designed an M-learning curriculum framework that attempted systematically and comprehensively to discover how and where mobiles should

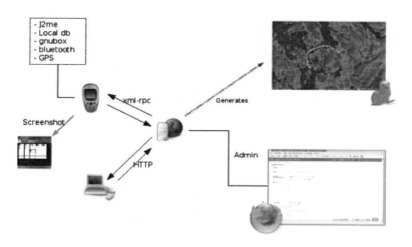

Figure 6.6. The MOTEL framework.

occur within educational provision [185].

The M-learning curriculum framework was set out as a varied and fairly high-level description of motivational material. The MLCF was presented through three broad learning environments to:

- learn about M-learning,
- be able to facilitate M-learning and
- understand the implications of M-learning implementation.

Each of the points mentioned above was linked to outcomes mapped to different competency levels. The assessment was specified through the implementation process. Figure 6.8 shows the methodology followed to design and produces the curriculum framework.

During Phase 1, a work team was formed, and a process for negotiation, methodology, scope and target audience defined. Phase 2 highlights and reviews experts according to their communities of practice. Phase 3 targets particular practitioner communities with a trace record of applying M-learning in formal and informal settings. Phase 4 involves a number of regional workshops, implemented to create awareness of collaboration and expose the curriculum

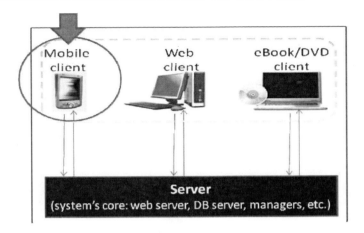

Figure 6.7. M-learning Framework for an Analog Electronics Course.

framework to a regional critique. Phase 5 aims to develop sample course-ware for accreditation, and to work towards integration.

Al-Bahadili proposed a hierarchical framework for evaluating success factors associated with M-learning [186]. Their framework evaluated the development and deployment of M-learning using a quantitative technique (analytic hierarchy process (AHP), such as the conventional AHP, fuzzy AHP (FAHP), fuzzy extend analysis (FEA), and alpha cut based).

The framework was divided into three levels; the first level comprising the main system criteria (mobile devices, quality, and learners' requirements or constraints). Each was further classified into a number of sub-criteria (level two), and each sub-criteria was then further divided into sub-sub-criteria (level three). While the other constrains have three levels, the requirements for the learners' constraints are only two level, as illustrated in Figure 6.9.

Mobile device constraints, quality of services and applications, and learners' requirements are the critical components considered in the development and deployment of M-learning. The main criteria for the proposed hierarchical framework are as shown in Figure 6.10.

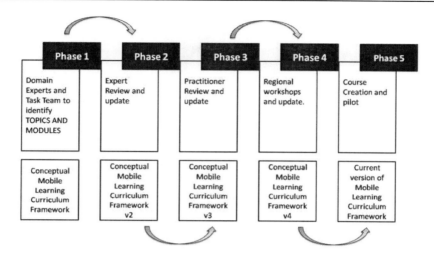

Figure 6.8. Phases in Creation of the Current Version Mobile Learning Curriculum.

- Mobile device constraints include software, hardware and network constraints. The constraints related to this component are shown in Figure 6.11.

- Quality of services and applications, the quality of the design is concerned with the design and quality of conformity with implementation. Quality in the ISO 9126 standard concerns functionality, usability, portability, efficiency, reliability and maintainability.

- Learners' requirements can be decompiled into the identification of learners' needs, structuring of pedagogical material, enhancement of the M-Learning environment, motivation for learner participation, tutorials. M-learning should be able to offer learners a basic problem solving mechanism, collaborative mechanisms, supportive tools and a combination of learning processes that support analysis, collaboration, synthesis, judging, problem solving, reasoning, evaluation and relations [195].

Park designed a pedagogical framework for M-learning: categorizing educational applications and mobile technologies into four types [187]. The framework provided used several elements of activity theory, to modify transactional

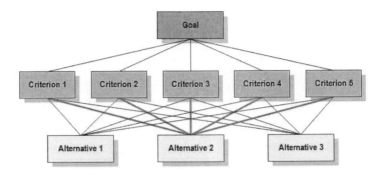

Figure 6.9. Standard Hierarchical Framework.

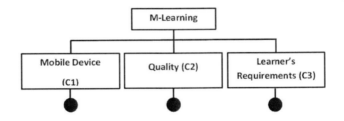

Figure 6.10. The main criteria of proposed M-Learning framework.

distance theory, adding a dimension and create a pedagogical framework for M-learning, as illustrated in Figure 6.14.

First, activity is conceived of as a unit of analysis, since transactional distance theory considers a learning program to include several lessons. Second, socialized and individualized activities are mediated by information and communication technologies, as one kind of cultural-historical artifact in activity theory. Third is the dichotomy of the individual versus society.

Boyinbode described an opencast M-learning framework for enhancing learning in higher education and explaining the evolution of podcasts to opencast [188]. Their framework helps postgraduate students in higher education to adapt educational resources from Opencast materials to their mobile devices, to be accessed anywhere at any time. Postgraduate students in higher education should be able to make use of their time for quality learning. Therefore, Opencast M-learning (OMLS) is valuable for supporting these students. The architecture depicted in Figure 6.15 illustrates how opencast M-learning enhances

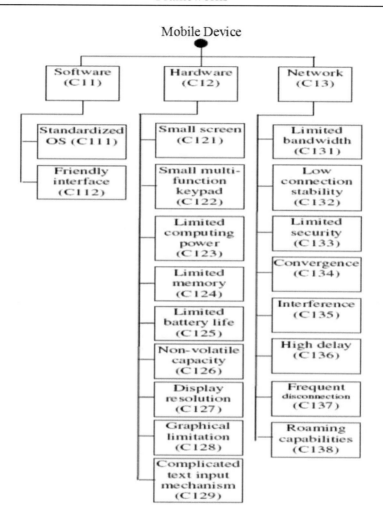

Figure 6.11. Mobile Device Constraints.

students' learning.

Berking proposed a new framework to support M-learning content within an instructional design (ID) model, with the use of traditional the ADDIE model as starting point [189]. Their framework is intended to inject concepts, guidelines, considerations and decisions that are specific to M-learning, into suitable points

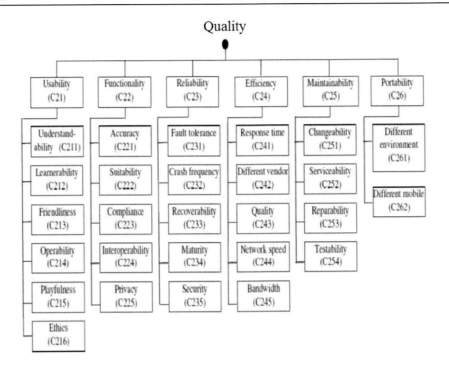

Figure 6.12. Quality of services and applications.

in the ID model. The framework design also accounts for performance support solutions, as a component of blended or independent approaches. Figure 6.16 describes advanced distributed learning M-learning framework phases.

Hendrik proposed a form of M-learning in a contextual framework, to capture the available intrinsic and extrinsic contextual information, and to combine everything into a standardized context model [41]. Their proposed framework, as shown in Figure 6.17, consists of two main components: context capturing and context modelling. Capture of the context can be done according to the environmental and activity sensors available. These include mobile devices and technologies, as well as the applications and services used by learners. The context modelling component is provided to process the sensor data received. Initially, all context information is gathered, analyzed, and adapted. Then, it can be categorized into different sets of intrinsic or extrinsic contextual information, which support combinations of single sensor data in a complete sensor

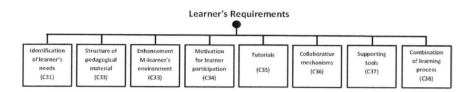

Figure 6.13. Learners Requirements.

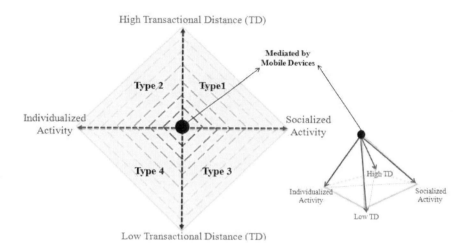

Figure 6.14. Four types of mobile learning: A pedagogical framework.

data set, reflecting a complete picture of the learners' contextual information. After which, a standardized context model can be generated.

All the aforementioned types of M-learning frameworks sought to address specific concerns including concept, conversation, requirements, design, social interaction, pedagogical and evaluation. However, the M-learning field still lacks a comprehensive framework that addresses the main influences in the development, adoption and dissemination of M-learning initiatives.

Despite the huge potential and many benefits that could be gained from using mobile technologies in educational systems, many challenges remain that influence the development, adoption and dissemination of M-learning including:

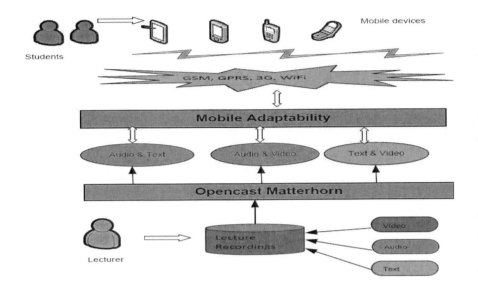

Figure 6.15. Architecture of Opencast Mobile Learning System (OMLS).

- Educational factors, e.g. mobile educational content, effect of mobile technology on the educational methods, what and how traditional educational content can be transferred to mobile, etc.

- Social and cultural concerns e.g. user behaviors (instructors, students, administrators, etc.), user awareness and acceptance, managing change, cost of network services required to access and system interact ... etc.

- Architecture and design of M-learning systems, which imply a lot of work to collect users' requirements and specify technical and non-technical requirements, in addition to defining the integration and interaction of different M-learning system components.

- Accessibility and look and feel are very important for successful M-learning system development and adoption, with the small size of mobile devices given and the typically lower functionality, compared with desktop computers.

- Trust, Privacy, and Copyright issues e.g. trust of mobile applications and

Frameworks

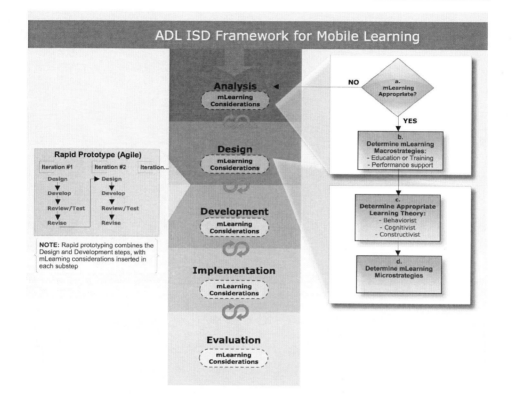

Figure 6.16. ADL Mobile Learning Framework.

privacy of the M-learning system in use, the confidentiality of the users sensitive data such as their grades, personal information, the copyright of the learning materials, etc.

- Mobile-inherited challenges, such as mobility of users, mobile network support (bandwidth) required to establish successful M-learning system.

- Compatibility issues, because different users have different kind of mobile devices with different capabilities/functionalities and operating systems.

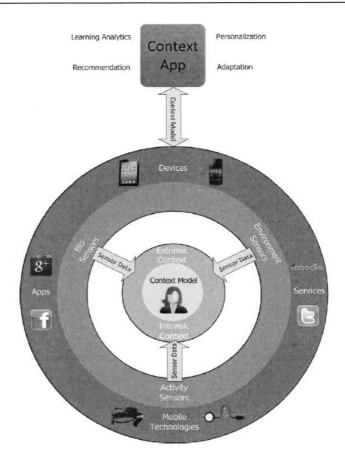

Figure 6.17. Mobile Learning in Context Framework.

6.4. Summary

This chapter has discussed all aspects related to M-learning frameworks. It has provided an overview of existing M-learning frameworks and introduced the different components of M-learning frameworks. It has critically discussed different M-learning frameworks including conversational frameworks for the effective use of learning technologies; a framework for M-learning systems based on educational components; a design requirements framework for M-

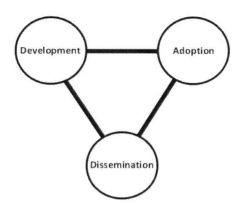

Figure 6.18. Main Components of Comprehensive M-learning Framework.

learning environments; M-learning: a framework and evaluation, a model for framing M-learning; MOTEL: a M-learning framework for Geo-Tagging and explorations of sites for learning; M-learning framework for an analog electronics course; MLCF: the M-learning curriculum framework; A hierarchical framework for evaluating M-learning success factors; a pedagogical framework for M-learning: categorizing educational the applications of mobile technologies into four types; an Opencast M-learning framework for enhancing learning in higher education; an ADL M-learning framework; Mobile Learning: Not Just Another Delivery Method and conceptual framework for context-aware M-learning.

Chapter 7

M-Learning in Education

Objectives

- Discusses M-learning applications in Education.
- Lists different technical factors that might influence the development and improvement of M-learning applications.
- Highlights the most common non-technical barriers to M-learning development, adoption and dissemination.

7.1. Introduction

This chapter discusses different M-learning applications in the Education sector and identifies principal requirements as introduced in chapter 5. Section 7.2 discusses the use of different M-learning applications in education. These application domains include various education and training providers: higher education providers, training and research centers, and basic schools. The main characteristics of the M-learning application reflect the needs of higher education, as discussed in section 7.4. Section 7.5 discusses the main concerns of the research and training centers' in reference to M-learning. Section 7.3 discusses the main M-learning requirements for the basic schools. Section 7.7 lists different technical factors that might influence development and result in improvements to M-learning applications. Section 7.8 highlights the most common non-technical barriers to M-learning development, adoption and dissemination.

7.2. The Use of M-Learning in Education

M-learning in education can be understood simply as a form of learning that uses mobile devices as a learning tool to support students and provide learning materials. It also facilitates access to learning materials, to help instructors deliver the required knowledge to students. A primary factor influencing the use of mobile devices as learning tools is the role of learning instructors. They are crucial in the success of any education system and learning innovation.

Instructors have to be skilled enough, and have the necessary ability to, utilize the different learning tools to effectively transmit knowledge and improve students learning ability. To date some schools, higher education providers, and training centers, have adopted M-learning technologies. Thus, many projects and research studies [196] have been conducted to evaluate M-learning from identifiable theoretical perspectives, and to determine implementations for M-learning. For example, UK higher education providers prompt teachers to use Short Messaging Services to meet course requirements and quizzes.

Studies have reported that the majority of available mobile devices can be used to store and retrieve learning information; e.g. timetables, course materials and e-books, etc. The more common findings of projects and research studies show how learning instructors can create learning content, and help students to receive or retrieve useful information. The next sections present an overview of M-learning experiences from different education providers, with the aim of sharing experiences and highlighting the main requirements of M-learning in education and at training institutions [197].

7.3. Basic Schools

Most basic infant and junior schools, i.e. pre-, primary and secondary schools, currently use networked computers to share lesson plans between management and staff. Some schools have up to date websites, which use embedded photos, videos and news feeds. These websites are typically static and weak in terms of security, because school networks are password protected. Access is controlled by requiring one password for each class. The computers on which the system can be accessed are usually located in schools. Each staff member has a password and can access folders over the schools network. The integrity of such systems is, therefore, a major requirement when assessing the risks associated with relying upon an M-learning application. This is because staff should be able to modify content over the schools network when authorized to do so. Another important factor when using M-learning applications in infant and junior schools is the opportunity for communication between schools and parents.

Modern mobile technologies support communications between parents and early year education providers, e.g. using text messages, emails, VoIP and other types of social network. Thus, flexibility and ease of use are very important characteristics, supporting effective communication between busy parents and their children's schools. Insuring the ready availability of M-learning application services can be a very important factor in maintaining the satisfaction and interest of students, staff and parents who use these services, e.g. the transition period between pre- and primary schools and between primary and secondary schools can often disrupt a child's education. Effective learning does not take place in chunks. M-learning applications can help reduce this disruption. Ensuring a quick response is another important factor in the provision of successful M-learning, e.g. teachers quick responses to parents' inquiries are very important with respect to students performances.

Moreover, when online games are integrated into lessons using multi-player, the participants must quickly reflect the actions of each player. Earlier years education providers can rely on the cloud to avoid the need to own high-cost of servers and network infrastructures. It seems, however, due to the lack of technical knowledge M-learning services are rarely implemented in infant or junior schools, and only a small web presence is found.

7.4. Higher Education Providers

Higher education providers incorporated several departments and sections with various responsibilities and duties, which in many cases, depended on expensive and large IT infrastructures to support their work. These departments could be situated in different locations. In fact, the actual use of their large and expensive fixed IT equipment was on average very low. Higher educational institutions recognize that adopting the latest technologies and solutions is essential if they are to remain competitive and retain students.

Using M-learning can help institutions and universities to reduce their high expenditure on software, hardware and maintenance. M-learning applications support virtual data centers that are accessible to faculty and admissions members, e.g. the required data can be accessed easily at any time and in any location. M-learning approaches enable higher education providers to concentrate on required services, rather than spending time dealing with IT operational and availability issues.

Higher education institution operations involve handling sensitive data, which includes grades and student information. Hence, prioritizing confidentiality, privacy and information flow control are essential requirements when assessing the risks associated with relying upon M-learning services. Learning resources and al deliverable content must be secured and well protected against attacks or unauthorized access. In addition, M-learning service data and applications should be accessible at all times. Hence, availability is one of the most important characteristics of M-learning applications.

7.5. Research and Training Centers

Data analysis, simulation tools, visualization and other important applications are essential to most field studies and research activities. Successful research outcomes always depend on the use of analytical methods, correct data management systems and high performance software tools and IT infrastructures. The cost of an IT infrastructure is often high and may be unaffordable for small laboratories and research groups. In addition, the need for IT equipment and its computations is not always continuous. The need to use IT is often based upon demand, which then depends on rate and experimental research work outcomes. Research centers and laboratories do not have to own complex IT infrastructures to provide M-learning services to analyze and compute large-scale data sets.

The extreme flexibility required for M-learning offers transformative and new usage modalities for training and research. For example, the system can help to insure submission deadlines are met, because students who use computers are more likely to finish their work early. Once they have submitted their papers these facilities can then be switched off. This renders the cost almost nothing compared to that when using normal IT equipment. M-learning allows training centers, researchers and students to best utilize their isolated working environments. The system will enable them to install their own M-learning applications, run jobs without contention and break things without risk. In addition, students and researchers can save the data on their virtual machine to perform or extend their analysis for other use. M-learning services also support team collaboration. Students and researchers can create a temporary shared development workspace, without risking security, by providing access to equipment that is jointly used. Students and researchers require a flexible data access mechanism from servers outside their offices and research laboratories. Thus, availability and mobile work lifestyles at training centers and research laboratories are crucial.

7.6. Characteristics of M-Learning in Education

Analysis of different M-learning applications in education, including higher education institutions, research and training centers and basic schools, illustrate use of the following characteristics for incorporating M-learning into various Educational and learning environments.

- Familiarity of mobile technology, it is important to support learners to explore and become familiar with the educational affordance and the technological features of mobile devices.

- Personally and collaboratively, M-learning can be used individually and collaboratively; whereas, the knowledge acquired can be provided individually or shared and discussed collaboratively with other learners.

- Produce and consume knowledge, M-learning should be used to assist learners to produce and consume the required knowledge. Well-constructed learning content will motivate learners and instructors to adopt an M-learning approach.

- Authentic contexts, M-learning should be used in a real context; and issues, barriers and challenges associated with M-learning should be set in real world context.

- Mobility of learners, mobile technologies support learning on the move; whereas, other technologies such as desktop PCs and digital cameras do not. Thus, M-learning should be used in contexts where learners are mobile.

- Mobile and non-mobile technologies, M-learning should enable the use of mobile and non-mobile technologies, such as the use of a combination of both computer software and mobile technologies, to develop, deliver and share the required learning material.

- Mobile technology features, different mobile technologies are suitable for different purposes because of the various capabilities of mobile technologies, such as the differences between cameras and mobile phones in terms of image resolution.

There are many technical and non-technical factors and challenges associated with the M-learning initiatives that are engaged in when attempting to adopt M-learning in Education. [198]

7.7. Technical Barriers

There are different technical factors that might influence developments and improvements to M-learning applications. The most common technical barriers to M-learning adoption are:

- Infrastructure is the most important technical barrier to M-learning development and adoption, including the speed and high cost of the Internet.

- M-learning Development Method, the developed application should consider application usability, ease of finding the required information, provide complete information to achieve higher M-learning take-up rates.

7.8. Non-technical Barriers

Non-Technical barriers have a substantial effect on the development, adoption and dissemination of M-learning. Non-Technical factors have different levels of impact. The following are the most common Non-Technical barriers:

- Ministry strategy, supports and improves the use of mobile devices as learning tools. The education ministry should have long term plans to improve staff and learners' abilities to use modern mobile technology as supporters of traditional learning systems.

- Decision maker support, support and understanding from the leadership is very important to the successful development of M-learning systems. Decision makers might see M-learning as a threat to their power, as it is perceived as similar to traditional learning systems.

- Learners expectations, high learner expectations can put pressure on the learning system and decision makers. Decision makers should be aware of the challenge brought about by new mobile technologies as these technologies are continually improving.

- Learners needs and involvement is important and central to M-learning development and adoption. Lack of users' knowledge, support and motivation in the area of mobile technology may effect M-learning development and adoption.

- Learners' trust is concerned with belief in the efficacy and security of learning materials provided through education M-learning systems, and also relates to how trustworthy and honest the learners interacting using the M-learning system are.

- Culture, learners' culture and behavior is critical in the development, adoption and dissemination of M-learning. As cultural issues differ from one nation to another, especially in the field of mobile computing.

- Demographics, the levels of ICT and mobile technologies knowledge, education and income among local society are crucial factors that might affect M-learning take-up in the Education system. In some cases poor learners might be unable to access M-learning services because of their cost.

- Resistance to change, another major challenge for M-learning adoption and dissemination that needs to be addressed is the tendency of learners to resist change, especially if these changes require extra effort.

- Security and privacy are very important issues in M-learning development and adoption. M-learning initiatives must be secure enough to overcome internal or external interference that might negatively affect the development and adoption of M-learning [199, 200].

Recently, Lucke and Resing [201] provided a review of the M-learning field, with the aim of specifying current trends and future challenges in M-learning. They specify challenges across two dimensions; first, those that include different levels of context-awareness, involving (location, activity, object, learner identity, device and network) and educational settings, involving (physical, collaborative, formalized settings and others).

The authors did not sufficiently stress the software engineering aspects required to support M-learning development, although they mentioned hardware and software dimensions in the classification they provided. Initial work was described by [202, 203], focusing on software engineering related aspects of M-learning. Software engineering methods for interoperability, platforms for scalability and deployment strategies for robust scalable applications were all identified as future issues and challenges to be addressed. Another challenge mentioned was to support resource sharing, including data, resources and other learning objectives, prompting the use of distributed solutions with mobile technology. However, the challenge is to provide an M-learning system architecture in which data and resources can be shared during execution.

7.9. Summary

This chapter has discussed the main concerns relating to M-learning in the Education system. It has discussed the number of M-learning applications in the Education sector, and the main characteristics of M-learning application designed for higher education. The chapter also discussed research and training centers' M-learning main concerns. It discussed primary and secondary schools main M-learning requirements. It also listed the different technical factors might influence the development and improvement of M-learning applications. The chapter also highlighted the most common non-technical barriers to M-learning development, adoption and dissemination.

Chapter 8

Summary

Objectives

- Summary of the contents of the book.
- Highlight existing M-learning issues.
- Suggest future directions for M-learning.

8.1. Summary of the Book

The purpose of this book was to explore all aspects of M-learning, including introducing different kinds of mobile operating systems, technical and non-technical requirements, components and frameworks, and explaining the use of M-learning in Education. I am certain that the simple and detailed introduction to M-learning presented in this book will provide the reader with a deeper understanding of all aspects of M-learning, encouraging the creative use of mobile devices as learning tools.

The book initially discussed the principles of learning and teaching; provided an introduction to the principles of traditional learning and related methods and components; and gave an overview of distance learning techniques, and highlighted the different advantages and challenges associated with these. In addition, it discussed different virtual learning forms; introduced different meanings and interpretations of E-learning and highlighted its diverse advantages. It also presented the meaning of ubiquitous learning and discussed its characteristics. In addition, it discussed the relationship between mobile technology and different learning approaches, with a focus on the use of mobile technologies in learning, as an approach to promoting interactive learning activities and increasing learners' motivation. Chapter 3 provided a general overview of mobile computing and discussed the main aspects of mobility, including user mobility and device portability. The chapter also described the principal components of mobile computing including mobile communication, mobile hardware and mobile software. It then focused on the mobile application development platforms including the most well-known mobile operating systems Iphone OS, Android, Symbian, Windows, Meego, Plam WebOS, Bada, LiMo, Blackberry and PyS60.

The objective of chapter 4 was to discuss different M-learning definitions and to present a theoretical background, provide an overview of M-learning characteristics and methods and present M-learning components. The chapter also provided a general overview of M-learning characteristics and methods, including formal, less formal and informal M-learning methods. It presented the four main M-learning components: learner, mobile device, learning material and mobile app. Chapter 5 provided an overview of M-learning applications. It discussed different M-learning requirements. It provided an introduction to the four different requirements of M-learning applications. It also discussed pedagogical and educational M-learning requirements and their different characteristics, including learning theories, instructional design models, quality of learning materials, completeness of learning materials, presentation of learning materials, organization of learning materials and learner Support. The chapter also discussed social and cultural M-learning requirements, including interaction, acceptability, visibility, sociability, attitude and intellectual property. This chapter also highlighted different business and economical M-learning requirements including cost, feasibility and cost-effectiveness. Finally it discussed various technical and Quality requirements, including availability, quick response, flexibility, scalability and security. The security requirements covered different important characteristics such as security completeness, data integrity, privacy, confidentiality and information flow control.

In chapter 6 all the aspects related to M-learning frameworks were discussed. It provided an overview of existing M-learning frameworks and introduced different M-learning framework components. It critically discussed different M-learning frameworks including the conversational framework for the effective use of learning technologies, a framework for an M-learning system based on educational components, a design requirements framework for M-learning environments, M-learning: a framework and evaluation, a model for framing M-learning, MOTEL: a M-learning framework for Geo-Tagging and explorations of sites for learning, an M-learning framework for an analog electronics course, MLCF: the M-learning curriculum framework, hierarchical framework for evaluating success factors of M-learning, a pedagogical framework for M-learning: categorizing educational applications of mobile technologies into four types, an Opencast M-learning framework for enhancing learning in higher education and ADL M-learning framework, Mobile Learning: Not Just Another Delivery Method.

Finally, chapter 7 discussed those aspects of M-learning causing concern within the Education system. It discussed a number of M-learning applications in the Education sector. The main characteristics of M-learning applications as designed for higher education were discussed. The chapter also discussed research and training centers' M-learning main concerns. It discussed primary and secondary schools main M-learning requirements and listed different technical factors that might influence the development and improvement of M-learning applications. The chapter highlighted the most common non-technical barriers to M-learning development, adoption and dissemination.

8.2. Open Issues and Future Direction

Mobile devices were found to share the following issues:

- Small screen.
- Battery power.
- Low connectivity.
- Poor input capabilities.
- Different mobile platforms.

Currently, tablet PCs are very different from those introduced a decade ago. They provided characteristics to support mobile hardware users, such as a large screen size, high resolution, different connectivity options and dynamic UI. The tablet PCs provided new mechanisms of human computer interaction sequences, such as code scanning, image recognition and multi-touch interfaces. As a result the review found out that M-learning methods shared constraints with distance learning, virtual learning and E-learning approaches, including technical support issues, isolation issues and lack of interaction between teachers and learners. However, the rapid improvements in mobile device technologies enhanced users abilities to take the learning process a step further with the benefit of anytime and anywhere access to learning materials, enhancing educator-centered learning, enhancing interaction between instructors and learners, just-in-time learning. In M-learning research, future directions are understood to raise a number of challenges, such as:

- Developing an M-Learning app to function across mobile platforms.
- Finding the best M-learning infrastructures.
- Creating a common user interface for M-learning.
- M-learning might make it easier for learners to cheat.
- There could be concerns among mobile learners with regard to trusting the wireless network.
- Design and development of an effective context aware M-learning app.
- The need for an additional learning curve for non-technical learners.

Author

Dr. Mohammed Sarrab has a Ph.D. in Computer Science and is currently working as research associate at CIRC (Communication and Information Research Center), Sultan Qaboos University, Muscat, Sultanate of Oman. His research interests are in areas of mobile applications, mobile learning (M-learning), E-learning and the use of information and communication technology in training and education. He is also interesting in computer security, runtime verification, information flow control, computer forensic and open source software. Dr. Sarrab is a member of ACM, IEEE, the IEEE Computer Society, IEEE Communications Society.

References

[1] Monica N. Nicolescu and Maja J. Mataric. Natural methods for robot task learning: Instructive demonstrations, generalization and practice. In *Second International Joint Conference on Autonomous Agents and Multi-Agent Systems*, pages 11–18, Melbourne, VIC, Australia, 2003. ACM New York, NY, USA.

[2] Jeanne Ellis Ormrod. *Human Learning*. Pearson London, London UK, 6th edition, 2011.

[3] David Eppstein. *Learning Spaces*, chapter Learning sequences, pages 43–59. Springer, Springer Heidelberg Dordrecht London New York, 2008.

[4] Joi L. Moore, Camille Dickson-Deane, and Krista Galyen. e-learning, online learning, and distance learning environments: Are they the same? *Internet and Higher Education*, 14:129-135, 2011.

[5] Tsvetozar Georgiev, Evgenia Georgieva, and Angel Smrikarov. M-learning - a new stage of e-learning. In *International Conference on Computer Systems and Technologies - CompSysTech-2004*, pages 1–5, Rousse, Bulgaria, 2004. Office of naval research international field office.

[6] Alex Sinclair. *Mobile education landscape report*. Technical report, GSMA Mobile Education, London, UK, 2011.

[7] Mohamed Ally. *State of Mobile Learning in Canada and Future Direction*. PhD thesis, Athabasca University, 2011.

[8] Nadire Cavus and Dogan Ibrahim. m-learning: An experiment in using sms to support learning new english language words. *British Journal of Educational Technology*, 40(1):78–91, 2008.

[9] McConatha Douglas, Praul Matt, and Lynch Michael J. Mobile learning in higher education: An empirical assessment of a new educational tool. *Turkish Online Journal of Educational Technology*, 7(3):15–21, 2008.

[10] Mohamed Sarrab, Laila Elgamel, and Hamza Aldabbas. Mobile learning (m-learning) and educational environments. *International Journal of Distributed and Parallel Systems*, 3(4):31–38, 2012.

[11] Orlando R. E. Pereira and Joel J. P. C. Rodrigues. Survey and analysis of current mobile learning applications and technologies. *ACM Computing Survey*, 46(2):1–35, 2013.

[12] Steinar Kristoffersen and F Ljungberg. Mobility: From stationary to mobile work. In *Planet Internet (2000)*, pages 41–64, Lund, Sweden, 2000. Studentlitteratur.

[13] Cohen Albert. Japan loves wireless. *PC Magazine*, 21(8):136, 2002.

[14] Patricia Thornton and Chris Houser. Using mobile phones in education. In *IEEE International Workshop on Wireless and Mobile Technologies in Education*, pages 3–8, JungLi, Taiwan, 2004. IEEE Computer Society, Washington, DC, USA.

[15] Shahid Islam Wains and Waqar Mahmood. Integrating m-learning with e-learning. In *9th ACM SIGITE conference on Information technology education*, pages 31–38, Cincinnati, OH, USA, 2008. ACM New York, NY, USA.

[16] Sheldon J. Lachmana. Learning is a process: Toward an improved definition of learning. *Journal of Psychology: Interdisciplinary and Applied*, 131(5):477–480, 1997.

[17] Michael Domjan. *Principles of learning and behavior*. Cengage Learning, Cengage Learning , KY, USA, 7th edition, 2014.

[18] Jan De Houwer. Why the cognitive approach in psychology would profit from a functional approach and vice versa. *Perspectives on Psychological Science*, 6:202–209, 2011.

References

[19] Jan De Houwer, Dermot Barnes-Holmes, and Agnes Moors. What is learning? on the nature and merits of a functional definition of learning. *Psychonomic Bulletin & Review: Springer*, 20(4):631–642, 2013.

[20] Joseph D. Novak. Learning, creating, and using knowledge: Concept maps as facilitative tools in schools and corporations. *Journal of e-Learning and Knowledge Society*, 6(3):21–30, 2010.

[21] Haryadi Sarjono, Sevenpri Candra, and Nugroho Setiadi. From traditional learning into e-learning: Comparing students response to promote e-learning in college education. In *Proceedings of IEEE International Conference on Teaching, Assessment, and Learning for Engineering (TALE2013), IEEE Xplore,*, pages 7–11,, Bali Dynasty Resort, Kuta, Indonesia, 2013. IEEE.

[22] Mohamed Sarrab and Laila Elgamel. Contextual m-learning system for higher education providers in oman. *World Applied Sciences Journal*, 22(10):1412–1419, 2013.

[23] Roger Rist and Sue Hewer. *LTDI: Implementing Learning Technology*, chapter What is learning technology? Some definitions, pages 3–5. Learning Technology Dissemination Initiative, Institute for Computer Based Learning, Heriot Watt University, Edinburgh, UK, 1996.

[24] Mohamed Sarrab, Al-Shihi Hafedh, and Rehman Osama. Exploring major challenges and benefits of m-learning adoption. *British Journal of Applied Science & Technology*, 3(4):826–839, 2013.

[25] Sheryl Burgstahler. *Universal design of instruction: Definitions, principles and examples.* Technical report, DO-IT, University of Washington, U.S. Department of Education, Washington, USA, 2009.

[26] Sheryl Burgstahler. Universal design: Implications for computing education. *ACM Transaction. Computing. Education.*, 11(3):19, 2011.

[27] Robert Joan and S. P. Denisia. Features of electronic learning, mobile learning and virtual learning. *International Journal of Scienctific Research*, 2(4):73–75, 2013.

[28] iNACOL. *Fast facts about online learning, key k-12 online learning stats.* Technical report, International Association for K-12 Online Learning, 1934 Old Gallows Road, Suite 350 Vienna, 2013.

[29] Bowu Yan, Shengli Mao, and Li Ruan. Research on e-learning and its related issues. In *In proceedings of the 3rd IEEE International Conference on Computer Science and Information Technology (ICCSIT'10)*, volume 8, pages 331–334, Chengdu, China, 2010. IEEE.

[30] Sakina Sofia Baharom. *Designing Mobile Learning Activities In The Malaysian He Context: A Social Constructivist Approach.* PhD thesis, Salford Business School, University of Salford, Salford, UK, February 2013.

[31] Jim Hillage Emma Pollard. *Exploring e-Learning*, volume 376. Institute for Employment Studies, Brighton, UK, 2001.

[32] Marc J. Rosenberg. *E-Learning: Strategies for Delivering Knowledge in the Digital Age.* McGraw-Hill, New York, 1 edition, 2000.

[33] Zoraini Wati Abas, Kuldip Kaur, and Hairuddin Harun. *E-learning readiness in malaysia: A joint study by ministry of energy, water and communication & open university malaysia.* Technical report, Open University Malaysia, Malaysia, 2004.

[34] Kim Svetlana and Yonglk-Yoon. Adaptation e-learning contents in mobile environment. In *Proceeding ICIS '09 Proceedings of the 2nd International Conference on Interaction Sciences: Information Technology, Culture and Human*, pages 474–479, New York, USA, 2009. ACM New York, NY, USA.

[35] N.Mallikharjuna Rao, C.Sasidhar, and V. Satyendra Kumar. Cloud computing through mobile-learning. *International Journal of Advanced Computer Science and Applications (IJACSA),*, 1(6):42–46, 2010.

[36] Mohamed Sarrab, Nasser Alalwan, and Ahmed Alzahrani. M-learning the next generation of education in cyberspace. In *International Congress of Science, Engineering and Technology*, volume 75, pages 642–645, Rio de Janeiro, Brazil, 2013. World and Academic of Science, Engineering and Technology.

References

[37] Nasser Alalwan, Ahmed Alzahrani, and Mohamed Sarrab. Future of education system with m-learning. In *22nd International Conference on Management of Technology, Science, Technology and Innovationin the Emerging Markets Economy*, pages 119–123, Porto Alegre, Brazil, 2013. AIMOT2013.

[38] Bill Cope and Mary Kalantzis. Ubiquitous learning: An agenda for educational transformation. *Ubiquitous Learning, University of Illinois Press*, 1:3–14, 2010.

[39] Choi Bong Ho and Hwang Hyun Sik. Introduction of u-learning system in statistics korea. In *2013 IASE / IAOS Satellite Conference*, page 1, Macao, August 2013. IASE / IAOS.

[40] Mark van 't Hooft, Karen Swan, Cook Dale, and Yimei Lin. *Ubiquitous computing in education*, chapter What is ubiquitous computing?, pages 3–17. Mahwah, New Jersey: Lawrence Erlbaum Associates, New Jersey, 2007.

[41] Thus Hendrik, Mohamed Amine Chatti, Esra Yalcin, Christoph Pallasch, Bogdan Kyryliuk, Togrul Mageramov, and Ulrik Schroeder. Mobile learning in context. *International Journal of Technology Enhanced Learning*, 4(5/6):332–344, 2012.

[42] David Perry. *Hand-held computers (pdas) in school.* Technical report, Becta ICT research, British Educational Communications and Technology Agency, Coventry, UK, 2003.

[43] Laura Naismith, Peter Lonsdale, Giasemi Vavoula, and Mike Sharples. *Report 11: Literature review in mobile technologies and learning.* Technical report, University of Birmingham, Birmingham, UK, 2004.

[44] Jill Attewell. *Mobile technologies and learning: A technology update and m-learning project summary.* Technical report, Technology Enhanced Learning Research Centre, Learning and Skills Development Agency, London, UK, 2005.

[45] McFarlane Angela, Roche Nel, and Triggs Pat. *Mobile learning: Research findings report to becta.* Technical report, British Educational Communications and Technology Agency (Becta), University of Bristol, UK, 2007.

[46] Victor Chang. Web service testing and usability for mobile learning,. In *International Conference on Networking, International Conference on Systems and International Conference on Mobile Communications and Learning Technologies (ICNICONSMCL'06)*, pages 2–21, Morne, Mauritius, 2006. IEEE.

[47] Ulrich Hoppe, Andreas Lingnau, Isabel Machado, Ana Paiva, Rui Prada, and Frank Tewissen. Supporting collaborative activities in computer integrated classrooms - the nimis approach. In *CRIWG'2000 - 6th International Workshop on Groupware*, pages 94–101, Madeira, Portugal, 2000. IEEE Computer Society.

[48] Chih-Yung Chang and Jang-Ping Sheu. Design and implementation of ad hoc classroom and eschoolbag systems for ubiquitous learning. In *Proceedings. IEEE International Workshop on Wireless and Mobile Technologies in Education, 2002*, pages 8 – 14, Sweden, 2002. IEEE.

[49] Tzu-Chien Liu, Hsue-Yie Wang, Jen-Kai Liang, Tak-Wai Chan, and Jie-Chi Yang. Applying wireless technologies to build a highly interactive learning environment. In *Proceedings IEEE International Workshop on Wireless and Mobile Technologies in Education, 2002*, pages 63 – 70, Sweden, 2002. IEEE.

[50] R.Y.L. Ting. The advanced mobile learning practices: Learning features and implications. In *Seventh IEEE International Conference on Advanced Learning Technologies, 2007. ICALT 2007.*, pages 718 –720, Taipei, Taiwan, 2007. IEEE.

[51] Hokyoung Ryu, R Brown, A Wong, and David Parsons. Personal learning organiser designing a mobile learning experience for university students,. In *The Conference on Mobile learning Technologies and Applications (MoLTA)*, pages 20–23, New Zealand, 2007. Routledge, UK.

[52] Chris Evans. The effectiveness of m-learning in the form of podcast revision lectures in higher education multimedia. *International Journal of Computers & Education.*, 50(2):491–498, 2008.

[53] Gary Woodill. *The motif project: Mobile learning survey report.* Technical report, Advanced Distributed Learning (ADL), 2013.

[54] Gustavo Zurita and Miguel Nussbaumw. A constructivist mobile learning environment supported by a wireless handheld network. *Journal of Computer Assisted Learning*, 20(4):235–243, 2004.

[55] Ming-Puu Chen and Jung-Chuan Yen. An evaluation of learners' satisfaction toward mobile learning, proc. sixth wseas int'l conf. applied computer science, vol. 6, pp. 382-388, 2007. In *Sixth World Scientific and Engineering Academy and Society (WSEAS) International Conference*, volume 6, pages 382–388, Hangzhou, China, 2007. WSEAS Press.

[56] Traxler John and Kukulska-Hulme Agnes. Evaluating mobile learning: Reflections on current practice. In *World Conf. Mobile and Contextual Learning (mLearn '05) Mobile technology: The future of learning in your hands*, pages 1–8, Cape Town, South Africa, 2005. Open University, Open Research Online.

[57] M.F. Verdejo, C Celorrio, E Lorenzo, and T Sastre. An educational networking infrastructure supporting ubiquitous learning for school students. In *Sixth IEEE International Conference. Advanced Learning Technologies*, pages 174–178, Kerkrade, Netherlands, 2006. IEEE.

[58] Hiroaki Ogata and Yoneo Yano. Context-aware support for computer-supported ubiquitous learning. In *Proceedings of the The 2nd IEEE International Workshop on Wireless and Mobile Technologies in Education (WMTE-04)*, pages 27–34, JungLi, Taiwan, 2004. IEEE Computer Society.

[59] Dan Corlett, Mike Sharples, Susan Bull, and Tony Chan. Evaluation of a mobile learning organiser for university students. *Journal Computer Assisted Learning,*, 21(3):162–170, 2005.

[60] Tomasz Imielinski. Mobile computing: Dataman project perspective. *Mobile Networks and Applications - Special issue on mobile computing and system services*, 1(4):359–369, 1996.

[61] Raminder Kaur. Introduction to mobile computing. *The Journal of Computer Science and Information Technology*, 4(1):83–87, 2006.

[62] Martin Maskarinec Kathleen Neumann. Mobile computing within a distributed deductive database. In *In Proceedings of the 1997 ACM Sympo-

sium on Applied Computing (SAC-97), page 318-322, New York, USA, 1997. ACM, New York.

[63] Gregory F. Welch. A survey of power management techniques in mobile computing operating systems. *Newsletter, ACM SIGOPS Operating Systems Review*, 29(4):47–56, 1995.

[64] Roger Wattenhofer. *Mobile computing*. Technical report, Distributed Computing Group, Zurich, Switzerland, 2004.

[65] Rashmi Padiadpu. *Towards mobile learning: A scorm player for the google android platform.* Master's thesis, University of Warwick, Coventry, United Kingdom, 2008.

[66] Hyrum Carroll, J. Kelly Flanagan, and Satish Baniya. A trace-driven simulator for palm os devices. In *IEEE International Symposium on Performance Analysis of Systems and Software, 2005. ISPASS 2005.*, page 157-166, Austin, TX, 2005. IEEE.

[67] Apple. *ios developer library.* Technical report, Apple, USA, October 2013.

[68] Roy Want. iphone: Smarter than the average phone. *IEEE Pervasive Computing*, 9(3):9–6, 2010.

[69] Orlando R. E. Pereira, Jollo M. L. P. Caldeira, and Joel J. P. C. Rodrigues. A symbian-based mobile solution for intra-body temperature monitoring. In *In Proceedings of the 2010 12th IEEE International Conference on e-Health Networking Applications and Services (HealthCom-10)*, page 316-321, Lyon, France, 2010. IEEE.

[70] Victor Matos and Rebecca Grasser. Building applications for the android os mobile platform: a primer and course materials. *Journal of Computing Sciences in Colleges*, (26)1:23–29, 2010.

[71] Google Technical Team. *Android.* http://code.google.com/android/. Technical report, Google, 2008.

[72] Farhad Soleimanian Gharehchopogh, Farzaneh Abbaspour, Maryam Tanabi, and Isa Maleki. Review and evaluation of performance measures in

the mobile operating systems. *International Journal of Scientific & Engineering Research*, 4(3):1–7, 2013.

[73] Allan Hammershoj, Antonio Sapuppo, and Reza Tadayoni. Mobile platforms, an analysis of mobile operating systems and software development platforms. In *CMI international conference on social networking and communities*, pages 1–22, Copenhagen, Denmark, 2009. CMI.

[74] Jo Stichbury. *Symbian OS Explained: Effective C++ Programming for Smartphones (Symbian Press)*. 8. John Wiley and Sons Inc, John Wiley & Sons Inc., 111 River Street, Hoboken, NJ 07030, USA, 1 edition, January 2005.

[75] Andrew Yu. *Mobile devices general overview*. Technical report, Information Services and Technology, Massachusetts Institute of Technology, Cambridge, USA, April 2006.

[76] Abraham Silberschatz, Peter B. Galvin, and Greg Gagne. *Operating System Concepts [Hardcover]*. Wiley, John Wiley & Sons Inc., 111 River Street, Hoboken, NJ 07030, USA, 8 edition, 2008.

[77] Scott Schwarzhoff. *Q2 mobile developer survey, tablets take center stage, point to the future of anywhere computing* Technical report, Appcelerator, 2010.

[78] Kush. *Introduction to meego*. Technical report, E-nova Technologies, India, 2011.

[79] Sean Buckley. *Palm os desktop howto*. Technical report, The Public's Library and Digital Archive, University of North Carolina at Chapel Hill, 2002.

[80] Frank Ableson and Mark Palmer. *Programming the palm os for embedded ir applications*. Technical report, Microchip Technology Inc., 2004.

[81] bada Developers. *Samsung's smartphone platform, smartphone for everyone*. Technical report, Bada, 2011.

[82] Masoud Nosrati, Ronak Karimi, and Hojat Allah Hasanvand. Mobile computing: Principles, devices and operating systems. *World Applied Programming*, 2(7):399–408, 2012.

[83] Vipin Kamboj and Hitesh Gupta. Mobile operating systems. *International Journal of Engineering Innovation & Research*, 1(2):169–174, 2012.

[84] Ben Morris, Manfred Bortenschlager, Jon Lansdell, Cheng Luo, and Michelle Somerville. *Introduction to bada A Developer's Guide*. A John Wiley and Sons, Ltd, Publication, The Atrium, Southern Gate, Chichester, West Sussex, PO19 8SQ, United Kingdom, 1 edition, 2010.

[85] Matt Hamblen. *Exclusive: Global forecast puts android ahead of iphone, blackberry, windows mobile*. Technical report, Computerworld, 2009.

[86] BlackBerry. *Blackberry blackberry developer zone*. Technical report, Blackberry. Retrieved November 12, 2013 from http://us.blackberry.com/developers/., 2011.

[87] Orlando R. E. Pereira, Joao Caldeira, and Joel J. P. C. Rodrigues. An advanced and secure symbian-based mobile approach for body sensor networks interaction. *International Journal of E-Health and Medical Communications (IJEHMC)*, 2(1):1–16, 2011.

[88] NokiaCorporation. *Pys60 library reference, release 1.4.4*. Technical report, Nokia, 2008.

[89] Anjum Najmi and Jennifer Lee. Why and how mobile learning can make a difference in the k-16 classroom? In *In I. Gibson et al. (Eds.), Proceedings of Society for Information Technology & Teacher Education International Conference*, pages 2903–2910, Chesapeake, VA: AACE, 2009. Society for Information Technology & Teacher Education International Conference.

[90] Amanda Lenhart. *Teens and mobile phones over the past five years: Pew internet looks back*. Technical report, Pew Research Center, Pew Internet & American Life Project., 2010.

[91] Gregor Kennedy, Kerri-Lee Krause, Terry Judd, Anna Churchward, and Kathleen Gray. *First year students' experiences with technology: Are they really digital natives* Technical report, University of Melbourne, Melbourne., 2006.

[92] Pamela Pollara. *Mobile Learning in Higher Education: A Glimpse And A Comparison Of Student And Faculty Readiness, Attitudes And Perceptions*. PhD thesis, Louisiana State University, 2011.

[93] John Traxler. Learning in a mobile age. *International Journal of Mobile and Blended*, 2(1):1–12, 2009.

[94] Ann Brown and Joe Campione. Psychological theory and the design of innovative learning environments: On procedures, principles, and systems. In *In L. Schauble & R. Glaser (Eds.) Innovations in learning: New environments for education*, pages 289–325, Hillsdale, NJ: Lawrence Erlbaum Associates, 1996. Hillsdale, NJ: Lawrence Erlbaum Associates.

[95] Gordon Pask. Minds and media in education and entertainment: Some theoretical comments illustrated by the design and operation of a system for exteriorizing and manipulating individual theses. In *In R. Trappl & G. Pask (Eds.). Progress in cybernetics and systems research*, volume 4, pages 38–50, London, 1975. Hemisphere Publishing Corporation.

[96] Robert L. Bowman. Life on the electronic frontier: The application of technology to group work. *The Journal for Specialists in Group Work*, 4(23):428–445, 1998.

[97] Silva S. Karayan and Judith A. Crowe. Student perceptions of electronic discussion groups. *T.H.E. Journal*, 24(9):69–71, 1997.

[98] Rena M. Palloff and Keith Pratt. *Lessons from the Cyberspace Classroom: The Realities of Online Teaching*. Jossey-Bass, United States, 1 edition, 2001.

[99] Tomh Brown. Beyond constructivism, exploring future learning paradigms. *Education Today*, 2:1–11, 2005.

[100] George Siemens. Connectivism: A learning theory for the digital age. *International Journal of Instructional Technology & Distance Learning*, 2(1):1–5, 2005.

[101] Yrjo Engestrom. *Learning by expanding: An activity-theoretical approach to developmental research Plastic Comb*. Orienta-Konsultit Oy, Helsinki, Finland, 1987.

References

[102] Mike Sharples, Josie Taylor, and Giasemi Vavoula. Towards a theory of mobile learning. In *4th World conference on mLearning, mLearning 2005*, volume 1, pages 1–9, Cape Town, South Africa, 2005. mLearning2005.

[103] Mike Sharples. *Big issues in mobile learning.* Technical report, Report. Nottingham: Kaleidoscope Research, Nottingham, UK, 2006.

[104] Clark Quinn. *mlearning: Mobile, wireless, in-your-pocket learning.* Technical report, Line Zine, Line Zine, 2000.

[105] Roger Riggs and Vandenbrink Mark. *Programming for Wireless Devices with the Java 2 Platform, Micro Edition.* Addison-Wesley Longman Publishing Co., Inc., Boston, MA, USA, 2001.

[106] Claire O'Malley, Giasemi N. Vavoula1, Josie Taylor, Mike Sharples, and Paul Lefrere. *Guidelibes for learning/teaching/tutoring in a mobile environment.* Technical report, MOBIlearn, UK, 2003.

[107] Anna Trifonova. *Mobile learning - review of the literature.* Technical report, UNIVERSITY OF TRENTO, Povo - Trento (Italy), 2003.

[108] Desmond Keegan. The incorporation of mobile learning into mainstream education and training. In *Proceedings of mLearn2005-4th World Conference of mLearning*, page 1, Cape Town, South Africa, 2005. Mobilearn.

[109] Rositsa Doneva, Nikolaj Kasakliev, and George Totkov. Towards mobile university campuses. In *International Conference on Computer Systems and Technologies - CompSysTech'2006*, volume VI of *3*, pages 1–6, University of Veliko Tarnovo, Bulgaria, 2006. CompSysTech-2006.

[110] Laurillard Diana. *Mobile learning towards a research agenda*, volume 1 of *Occasional Papers in Work-based Learning, incollection Pedagogical forms of mobile learning: framing research questions*, pages 151–173. WLE Centre, London, 9 2007.

[111] Mike Sharples, Josie Taylor, and Giasemi Vavoula. A theory of learning for the mobile age. *The Sage Handbook of Elearning Research, London*, 1:221–247, 2007.

[112] Shon. J.G. m-learning trends in korea. In *ISO/IEC JTC1/SC36 Open Forum*, page 1, Seoul, Korea, 2008. ISO/IEC.

[113] Mohamed Ally. *Mobile Learning: Transforming the Delivery of Education and Training*. Issues in Distance Education Series. Athabasca University Press., Athabasca, AB T9S 3A3, Canada, June 2009.

[114] Tracey Wilen-Daugenti. *Education Technology and Learning Environments in Higher Education*. Peter Lang International Academic Publishers; First printing edition, New York, NY 10006 USA, 2009.

[115] Yi Jin. Research of one mobile learning system. In *International Conference on Wireless Networks and Information Systems, 2009. WNIS '09*, pages 162 – 165, Shanghai, 2009. IEEE Explore.

[116] Yuan Jiugen, Xing Ruonan, and Wang Jianmin. Applying research of mobile learning mode in teaching. In *International Forum on Information Technology and Applications (IFITA)*, volume 3, pages 417 – 420, Kunming, 2010. IEEE Explore.

[117] ISO/IEC. *Information technology for learning, education and training - nomadicity and mobile technologies - part 2: Learner information model for mobile learning]*. Technical report, ISO (the International Organization for Standardization) and IEC (the International Electrotechnical Commission), 2011.

[118] Siobhan Thomas. Pervasive, persuasive elearning: Modeling the pervasive learning space. In *Third IEEE International Conference on Pervasive Computing and Communications Workshops, 2005. PerCom 2005 Workshops*, pages 332 – 336, Washington, DC, USA, 2005. IEEE Computer Society.

[119] John Traxler. Defining, discussion and evaluating mobile learning. the moving finger writes and having write. *International Review of Research in Open and Distance Learning*, 8(2):1–12, 2007.

[120] Kristine Peters. m-learning: Positioning educators for a mobile, connected future. *International Journal Of Research in Open and Distance Learning*, 8(2):1–17, 2007.

[121] Hyungsung Park. Design and development of a mobile learning management system adaptive to learning style of students. In *IEEE International Workshop on Wireless and Mobile Technologies in Education, 2005. WMTE 2005*, pages 67–69, University of Tokushima, JAPAN, 2005. IEEE.

[122] Sang Hyun Kim, Clif Mims, , and Kerry P. Holmes. An introduction to current trends and benefits of mobile wireless technology use in higher education. *AACE Journal*, 14(1):77–100, 2006.

[123] Margaret Maag. Podcasting and mp3 players: Emerging educational technology. *Computers,Informatics, Nursing*, 24(1):9–13, 2006.

[124] Jason G. Caudill. The growth of m-learning and the growth of mobile computing: Parallel developments. *International Review of Research in Open and Distance Learning*, 8(2):1–13, 2007.

[125] Catalin Boja and Lorena Batagan. Software characteristics of m-learning applications. In *Proceedings of the 10th WSEAS international conference on Mathematics and computers in business and economics*, pages 88–93, Stevens Point, Wisconsin, USA, 2009. World Scientific and Engineering Academy and Society (WSEAS).

[126] Douglas Mcconatha, Matt Praul, and Michael J. Lynch. Mobile learning in higher education: An empirical assessment of a new educational tool. *The Turkish Online Journal of Educational Technology*, Vol. 7(3)., 7(3):15–21, 2008.

[127] Sam Goundar. What is the potential impact of using mobile devices in education? In *Proceedings of SIG GlobDev Fourth Annual Workshop*, pages 1–30, Shanghai, China, 2011. GIS.

[128] Umer Farooq, Wendy Schafer, Mary Beth Rosson, and John M. Carroll. M-education: Bridging the gap of mobile and desktop computing. In *IEEE International Workshops on Wireless and Mobile Technologies in Education (WMTE'02)*, pages 91 – 94, Vaxjo, Sweden, 2002. IEEE Computer Society Washington, DC, USA.

[129] Eric Klopfer, Kurt Squire, and Henry Jenkins. Environmental detectives: Pdas as a window into a virtual simulated world. In *International Work-*

shop on Wireless and Mobile Technologies in Education,, pages 95 – 98, Vaxjo, Sweden, 2002. IEEE.

[130] Geoff Stead. Moving mobile into the mainstream. In *mLearn 2005: 4th World Conference on Mobile Learning*, pages 1–9, Cape Town, South Africa, 2005. mLearning2005.

[131] Thomas Cochrane and Roger Bateman. Smartphones give you wings: Pedagogical affordances of mobile web 2.0. *Australasian Journal of Educational Technology*, 26(1):1–14, 2010.

[132] Bryan Alexander. oing nomadic: Mobile learning in higher education. *EDUCAUSE Review*, 39(5):29–35, 2004.

[133] Bryan Patten, Inmaculada Arnedillo Snchez, and Brendan Tangney. Designing collaborative, constructionist and contextual applications for handheld devices. *Computers and Education*, 46(3):294-308, 2006.

[134] Agnes Kukulska-Hulme. Mobile usability in educational contexts - what have we learn? *Special issue of the International Review of Research in Open and Distance Learning*, 8(2):1–16, 2007.

[135] Matthew Kearney, Sandra Schuck, Kevin Burden, and Peter Aubusson. Viewing mobile learning from a pedagogical perspective. *Research in Learning Technology*, 20:1, 2012.

[136] Ouiame Filali Marzouki, Mohammed Khalidi Idrissi, and Samir Bennani. Towards a new mobile educational model, adaptation of the method for engineering learning systems misa. In *Proceedings of the 2013 International Conference on Education and Modern Educational Technologies*, pages 74–81, Venice, Italy, 2013. EMET 2013.

[137] Yuhsun Edward Shih and Dennis Mills. Setting the new standard with mobile computing in online learning. *The International Review of Research in Open and Distance Learning*, 8(2):1-16, 2007.

[138] Chi-Hong Leung and Yuen-Yan Chan. Mobile learning: a new paradigm in electronic learning. In *The 3rd IEEE International Conference on Advanced Learning Technologies, 2003. Proceedings*, pages 76 – 80, Athens, Greece, 2003. IEEE.

[139] David Parsons, Hokyoung Ryu, and Mark Cranshaw. A study of design requirements for mobile learning environments. In *Sixth International Conference on Advanced Learning Technologies*, pages 96–100, Kerkrade, 2006. IEEE.

[140] Masoud Hashemia, Vahid Najafia Masoud Azizinezhad and, and Ali Jamali Nesari. What is mobile learning? challenges and capabilities. *Procedia Social and Behavioural Sciences*, 30:2477–2481, 2011.

[141] Harri Alamaki and Pauliina Seppala. Experimenting with mobile learning in a university environment. In *World Conference on E-Learning in Corporate, Government, Healthcare, and Higher Education*, pages 67–74, Montreal, Canada, 2002. Association for the Advancement of Computing in Education (AACE), Chesapeake, VA.

[142] Jill Attewell and Mats Gustafsson. Mobile communications technologies for young adult learning and skills development (m-learning). In *IEEE International Workshop on Wireless and Mobile Technologies in Education, 2002. Proceedings*, pages 158 – 160, Vaxjo, Sweden., 2002. IEEE.

[143] Kathryn MacCallum and Lynn Jeffrey. Identifying discriminating variables that determine mobile learning adoption by educators: An initial study. In *Proceedings ascilite Auckland 2009: Concise paper: MacCallum and Jeffrey*, pages 602–608, The University of Auckland, 2009. The University of Auckland, Auckland University of Technology, and Australasian Society for Computers in Learning in Tertiary Education (ascilite).

[144] Nicola Louise Beddall-Hill. It's not what you know but the device you know: The influence of ownership on appropriation of mobile devices for learning in field trips. In *Proceedings of 2011 mobile learning: crossing boundaries in convergent environments conference,*, pages 27–29, Bremen, Germany,, 2011. London Mobile Learning Group.

[145] Jennifer Duncan-Howell and Kar-Tin Lee. M-learning: Finding a place for mobile technologies within tertiary educational settings. In *In ICT: Providing Choices for Learners and Learning. Proceedings ascilite Singapore*, pages 223–232, Singapore, 2007. ascilite Singapore.

[146] Anastasios A Economides. Adaptive context-aware pervasive and ubiquitous learning. *International Journal of Technology Enhanced Learning*, 1(3):169–192, 2009.

[147] Teemu H. Laine, Carolina A. Islas Sedano, Mike Joy, and Erkki Sutinen. Critical factors for technology integration in game-based pervasive learning spaces. *IEEE Transaction On Learning Technologies*, 3(4):294–306, 2010.

[148] Ferial Khaddage and Christoph Lattemann. iteach we learn via mobile apps a case study in a business course. In *In R. McBride & M. Searson (Eds.), Proceedings of Society for Information Technology & Teacher Education International Conference*, page 3225-3233, Chesapeake, VA: AACE., 2013. Society for Information Technology & Teacher Education International Conferenc.

[149] Kwok-Wing Lai, Ferial Khaddage, and Gerald Knezek. Working group 2: Advancing mobile learning across formal and informal contexts. In *International Summit on ICT Education, EDU SUMMIT2013*, pages 1–7, Washington D.C., United States of America., 2013. Edusummit.

[150] Mike Sharples, Dan Corlett, and Oliver Westmancott. The design and implementation of a mobile learning resource. *Personal and Ubiquitous Computing*, 6(3):220 – 234, 2002.

[151] Jill Attewell. From research and development to mobile learning: Tools for education and training providers and their learners. In *4th World Conference on mLearning.*, page 1, Cape Town, South Africa, 2005. mLearning.

[152] Kukulska-Hulme. *in Giasemi Vavoula; Norbert Pachler, Agnes Kukulska-Hulme, ed. Researching Mobile Learning: Frameworks, tools and research designs' Peter Lang AG*, chapter Conclusions: Future Directions in Researching Mobile Learning, pages 353–365. International Academic Publishers, Peter Lang Verlag, Oxford, UK, 2009.

[153] Claudio Zaki Dib. Formal, non-formal and informal education: Concepts/applicability. In *AIP Conference*, volume 173, pages 300 – 315, USA, 1988. American Institute of Physics.

[154] Irmeli Maunonen-Eskelinen. *Formal, non-formal, informal learning.* Technical report, Jyvaskyla University of Applied Sciences, Education College,, JAMK University of Applied Sciences, Rajakatu 35, 2007.

[155] Patrick Werquin. *Recognising non-formal and informal learning outcomes, policies and practices.* Technical report, Organisation For Economic Co-Operation And Development, Paris Cedex 16 Printed In France, 2010.

[156] Luiz Fernando Capretz. Clues on software engineers learning styles. *International Journal of Computing & Information Sciences*, 4(1):46–49, 2006.

[157] Richard M. Felder. Learning and teaching styles in engineering education. *ENGINEERING EDUCATION. Engr. Education*, 78(7):674–681, 1988.

[158] Abdalha Ali. *A framework for measuring the usability issues and criteria of mobile learning applications.* Master's thesis, The School of Graduate and Postdoctoral Studies, Western University,, London, Ontario, Canada, 2013.

[159] IBM. *Native, web or hybrid mobile-app development.* Technical report, IBM Corporation, Software Group, United States of America, 2012.

[160] Hinny P. Kong, William K. H. Lim, Lei Wang, and Robert Gay. Scmp: An e-learning content migration and standardization approach (a singaporean perspective). *Journal of Distance Education Technologies*, 4(2):1–9, 2006.

[161] Ben Adida. The mobile browser as a web-based platform for identity. In *Workshop on Mobile Ajax*, pages 1–3, ERCIM, Keio University, MIT CSAIL, 2007. W3C.

[162] Essa Basaeed, Jawad Berri, Mohamed Jamal Zemerly, and Rachid Benlamri. Learner-centric context-aware mobile learning. *IEEE Multidisciplinary Engineering Education Magazine*, 2(2):30–33, 2007.

[163] Wu Junqi, Qi Lili, and Zhengbing Hu. Notice of retraction 3g phone-based mobile learning for improving k-12 tearchers' educational technology in rural area. In *Second International Workshop on Education*

Technology and Computer Science (ETCS), pages 821 – 825, Wuhan, China, 2010. IEEE.

[164] Bhruthari Pund, Sanil Nair, and Prajakta Deshmukh. Using cloud computing on e-learning. *International Journal Of Emerging Trends & Technology In Computer Science (IJETTCS),*, 1(2):202–209, 2012.

[165] Xuefei Chen, Jing Liu, Jun Han, and Hongyun Xu. Primary exploration of mobile learning mode under a cloud computing environment. In *In the Proceedings of the 2010 International Conference on E-Health Networking, Digital Ecosystems and Technologies (EDT 2010)*, volume 2, pages 484–487, Shenzhen, China, 2010. IEEE.

[166] Antti Oulasvirta, Mikael Wahlstrom, and K. Anders Ericsson. What does it mean to be good at using a mobile device? an investigation of three levels of experience and skill. *International Journal of Human-Computer Studies*, 69(3):155–169, 2011.

[167] Anthony I Wasserman. Software engineering issues for mobile application development. In *in Proceedings of the FSE/SDP workshop on Future of software engineering research - FoSER -10*, pages 397–400, New York, NY, USA, 2010. ACM New York, NY, USA.

[168] Nathaniel Ostashewski and Doug Reid. ipod, iphone, and now ipad: The evolution of multimedia access in a mobile teaching context. In *In Proceedings of World Conference on Educational Multimedia, Hypermedia and Telecommunications, Chesapeake, VA: AACE*, pages 2862–2864, Toronto, Canada, 2010. EDITLiB.

[169] Anastasios Economides. Requirements of mobile learning applications. *International Journal of Innovation and Learning*, 5(5):457–479, 2008.

[170] Ahmed Alzahrani, Nasser Alalwan, and Mohamed Sarrab. Mobile cloud computing advantage, disadvantage and open challenge. In *Proceedings of the 7th Euro American Conference on Telematics and Information Systems*, number 21 in 1, pages 1–4, Valparaso, Chile, 2014. ACM New York, NY, USA.

[171] Steve Bigelow and Features Writer. *Understanding the impact of high-availability applications on the network.* Technical report, Search IT Channel (TechTarget), Newton, USA, 2008.

References

[172] Mohamed Sarrab. *Runtime Verification of Information flow: Policy-Based Runtime Verification of Information Flow Control*. LAP Lambert Academic Publishing, LAP, 2011.

[173] Mohamed Sarrab and Helge Janicke. Runtime monitoring and controlling of information flow. *International Journal of Computer Science and Information Security (IJCSIS).*, 8(9):37–45, 2010.

[174] Helge Janicke, Mohamed Sarrab, and Hamza Aldabbas. Controlling data dissemination. Springer, *Lecture Notes in Computer Science.*, 1(7122):303–309, 2012.

[175] Mohamed Sarrab, Helge Janicke, and Antonio Cau. Interactive runtime monitoring of information flow policies. In *Second international conference of Creativity and Innovation in software Engineering*, pages 1–8, Ravda (Nessebar), Bulgaria, 2009. STRL.

[176] Mohamed Sarrab and Helge Janicke. Runtime monitoring of information flow policies. In *Doctoral/PhD Workshop of 4th ACM International Conference on Distributed Event-Based Systems (DEBS-2010),.*, UK, 2009. ACM.

[177] Mohamed Sarrab. Runtime verification using policy-based approach to control information flow. *International Journal of Security and Networks (IJSN).*, 8(4):212–230, 2013F.

[178] Diana Laurillard. *A conversational framework for the effective use of learning technologies*. Technical report, Rethinking University Teaching., London: Routledge, 2002.

[179] Jari Mustajarvi Ali Mostakhdemin-Hosseini. Framework for mobile learning system based on education component. In *Proceedings of the International Conference on Theory and Applications of Mathematics and Informatics - ICTAMI 2003*, pages 191–196, Alba Iulia, 2003. ICTAMI.

[180] David Parsons, Hokyoung Ryu, and Mark Cranshaw. A design requirements framework for mobile learning environments. *JOURNAL OF COMPUTERS*, 2(4):1–8, 2007.

[181] Luvai F. Motiwalla. Mobile learning: A framework and evaluation. *Computers & Education*, 49:581-596, 2007.

[182] Marguerite Koole. A model for framing mobile learning. *Mobile learning: Transforming the delivery of education and training*, 1:25–47, 2009.

[183] Rune Baggetun. Motel: A mobile learning framework for geo-tagging and explorations of sites for learning, research and practice in technology enhanced learning. *World Scientific Publishing Company & Asia-Pacific Society for Computers in Education*, 4(1):83-107, 2009.

[184] Rui Neves Madeira, V. Fernao Pires, O. P. Dias, and J. F. Martins. Development of a mobile learning framework for an analog electronics course. In *IEEE EDUCON Education Engineering - The Future of Global Learning Engineering Education*, pages 561–567., Madrid Spai, 2010. IEEE EDUCON Education Engineering.

[185] Adele Botha. *Mlcf:the mobile learning curriculum framework*. Technical report, GreenZoner, Tangient LLC, Egypt., 2010.

[186] Hussein Al-Bahadili, Ghassan Issa, and Maher Abuhamdeh. A hierarchical framework for evaluating success factors of m-learning. *The Research Bullet of Jordan ACM*, II(III):46–51, 2010.

[187] Yeonjeong Park. A pedagogical framework for mobile learning: Categorizing educational applications of mobile technologies into four types. *The International Review of Research in Open and Distance Learning*, 12(2):78–102, 2011.

[188] Olutayo Boyinbode, Antoine Bagula, and Dick Ngambi. An opencast mobile learning framework for enhancing learning in higher education. *International Journal of u- and e- Service, Science and Technology*, 4(3):11–18, 2011.

[189] Peter Berking, Jason Haag, Thomas Archibald, and Marcus Birtwhistle. Mobile learning: Not just another delivery method. In *Interservice/Industry Training, Simulation, and Education Conference*, number 12079 in 1, pages 1–10, Orlando, Florida , U. S, 2012. (I/ITSEC) 2012.

[190] Josie Taylor, Mike Sharples, Claire O'Malley, Giasemi Vavoula, and Jenny Waycott. Towards a task model for mobile learning: a dialectical approach. *International Journal of Learning Technology*, 2:138–158, 2006.

[191] Gustavo Zurita and Miguel Nussbaum. A conceptual framework based on activity theory for mobile cscl. *British Journal of Educational Technology*, 38(2):211–235, 2007.

[192] Lorna Uden. Activity theory for designing mobile learning. *International Journal of Mobile Learning and Organization*, 1(1):81–102, 2007.

[193] Frohberg D and Goth C andSchwabe G. Mobile learning projects: a critical analysis of the state of the art. *Journal of Computer Assisted Learning*, 25(3):307–331, 2009.

[194] Donald Norman. Affordance, conventions and design. *Interactions*, 6(3):38–43, 1999.

[195] Maher AbuHamdeh and Adel Hamdan. Using analytical hierarchy process to measure critical success factors of m-learning. In *European, Mediterranean & Middle Eastern Conference on Information Systems*, pages 1–23, Abu Dhabi, UAE, 2010.

[196] Brian Ferry. Using mobile phones to enhance teacher learning in environmental education. *Research online University of Wollongong*, 1(1):45–55, 2009.

[197] Jan Herrington, Anthony Herrington, Jessica Mantei, Ian Olney, and Brian Ferry, editors. *New technologies, new pedagogies: Mobile learning in higher education*. Faculty of Education, University of Wollongong, 2009.

[198] Hafedh AlShihi. *Critical Factors in the Adoption and Diffusion of E-goverment Initiatives in Oman*. PhD thesis, School of Information systems, Faculty of Business and Law, Victoria University, 2006.

[199] Mohamed Sarrab and Hadj Bourdoucen. Runtime monitoring using policy based approach to control information flow for mobile applications. In *International Conference on Computer Applications*, 83, pages 1276–1283, Malaga, Spain, 2013. World Academy of Science, Engineering and Technolo.

[200] Mohamed Sarrab and Hadj Bourdoucen. Runtime monitoring using policy based approach to control information flow for mobile apps. *Interna-*

tional Journal of Communication Science and Engineering, 7(11):913–920, 2013.

[201] Ulrike Lucke and Christoph Rensing. A survey on pervasive education. *Pervasive and Mobile Computing*, 13(1):1, 2013.

[202] Oskar Pettersson and Bahtijar Vogel. Reusability and interoperability in mobile learning: A study of current practices. In *IEEE Seventh International Conference on Wireless, Mobile and Ubiquitous Technology in Education (WMUTE)*, pages 306 – 310, Takamatsu, 2012. IEEE.

[203] Lars Bollen, Marc Jansen, and Sabrina C. Eimler. Towards a multichannel input dimension in learning scenarios with mobile devices. In *IEEE Seventh International Conference on Wireless, Mobile and Ubiquitous Technology in Education (WMUTE)*, pages 311 – 315, Takamatsu, 2012. IEEE.

Index

A

abstraction, 24, 37, 53, 55
academic learning, 77
access, 2, 3, 13, 15, 16, 17, 18, 32, 35, 37, 38, 42, 43, 44, 45, 46, 47, 53, 58, 59, 63, 66, 69, 71, 72, 88, 94, 96, 99, 104, 125
accessibility, 11, 47, 51, 66, 71
accreditation, 82
activity theory, 76, 83, 128
adaptation, 121
administrators, 88
adult learning, 122
adults, 42
Africa, 121
age, 63, 69, 117, 118
AMF, 35
application component, 70
ARM, 28, 31
Asia, 127
assessment, 81, 108, 120
attitudes, 10
authentication, 71
awareness, 18, 47, 81, 88, 99

B

bandwidth, 68, 89
banking, 66
barriers, 2, 46, 93, 97, 98, 100, 103
base, 22
behaviorism, 61
behaviors, 10, 88
benefits, 1, 60, 64, 87, 109, 120
bile, 3, 5, 9, 16, 17, 29, 42, 43, 46, 47, 55, 88, 89, 97, 102, 108, 110, 111, 114
Bluetooth, 32, 39, 52
Brazil, 110, 111
browser, 54, 124
browsing, 54
Bulgaria, 107, 118, 126
businesses, 6

C

C++, 24, 27, 29, 32, 33, 35, 37, 38, 53, 115
case study, 123
cation, 11, 22, 37, 48, 64, 66, 67, 100
cell phones, 42
certification, 49, 71
challenges, 5, 9, 12, 19, 33, 60, 87, 89, 97, 98, 99, 100, 101, 104, 109, 122
chat rooms, 12
children, 42, 95
Chile, 125
China, 110, 113, 120, 125
classes, 3, 38
classification, 100
classroom, 1, 2, 3, 11, 12, 13, 14, 15, 17, 19, 48, 112, 116
cleanup, 39

collaboration, 15, 18, 48, 59, 62, 79, 81, 83, 96
colleges, 3
commerce, 34, 60, 79
commercial, 79
common findings, 94
communication, 2, 3, 4, 11, 12, 15, 17, 22, 23, 30, 32, 42, 43, 44, 46, 47, 52, 53, 58, 62, 67, 68, 69, 71, 95, 105
communication technologies, 2, 3, 4, 11, 17
communities, 28, 43, 81, 115
community, 43, 49
competitors, 24
computer, 5, 11, 12, 13, 14, 15, 16, 23, 42, 52, 60, 97, 103, 105, 112, 113
computer software, 97
computing, 4, 5, 12, 13, 16, 21, 22, 23, 28, 30, 31, 33, 39, 44, 52, 58, 99, 102, 109, 111, 113, 114, 115, 120, 121, 125
conference, 108, 115, 118, 120, 122
confidentiality, 6, 57, 70, 71, 72, 73, 89, 102
configuration, 66
conformity, 83
Congress, 31, 110
connectivity, 22, 24, 53, 56, 67, 79, 103
construction, 43
constructivism, 61, 117
consumers, 67
consumption, 33, 53, 59
convergence, 79
conversations, 44
copyright, 88, 89
cost, 6, 16, 42, 55, 57, 73, 78, 88, 95, 96, 98, 99, 102
CPU, 37
critical analysis, 128
cryptography, 71
CSS, 32, 53, 54, 55
culture, 99
curricula, 6
curriculum, 6, 48, 49, 75, 80, 81, 91, 103, 127
cyberspace, 110

D

data center, 66, 95
data communication, 22
data set, 87, 96
data structure, 33
database, 32, 35, 80, 113
decision makers, 99
demonstrations, 107
Denmark, 115
Department of Education, 109
detection, 34
developing countries, 3, 42
dichotomy, 84
digital cameras, 97
disaster, 23
disaster relief, 23
disclosure, 72
discussion groups, 117
distance learning, 2, 4, 5, 9, 59, 101, 107
distribution, 3, 26, 28, 29, 37, 38, 53
DOC, 53

E

economics, 46, 120
editors, 26, 128
education, 1, 2, 3, 5, 6, 7, 10, 11, 13, 15, 18, 42, 44, 47, 48, 49, 58, 59, 75, 76, 79, 93, 94, 95, 96, 97, 98, 99, 105, 107, 108, 109, 110, 111, 117, 118, 119, 120, 123, 126, 127, 128, 129
educational institutions, 95
educational objective, 10, 61
educational system, 87
educators, 10, 119, 122
Egypt, 127
electron, 51
electronic learning, 4, 109, 121
encryption, 71
energy, 68, 110
energy consumption, 68

Index

engineering, 60, 79, 100, 121, 124, 125
environment, 10, 14, 16, 24, 27, 32, 38, 44, 46, 47, 59, 67, 68, 83, 110, 113, 122, 125
environmental issues, 64
environments, 22, 29, 43, 45, 48, 49, 53, 78, 96, 107, 108, 117, 122
equipment, 95, 96
ester, 116
evolution, 84, 125
execution, 23, 30, 34, 55, 100

F

fabrication, 71
facilitators, 14, 48
fencing, 52
Finland, 117
firewalls, 71
flexibility, 6, 11, 17, 45, 47, 57, 59, 66, 67, 73, 95, 96, 102
formal education, 48
formation, 79
framing, 75, 79, 91, 103, 118, 127
France, 114, 124
freedom, 27, 59
functional approach, 108

G

Galaxy, 34, 53
Germany, 122
GIS, 120
google, 114
GPS, 18, 19, 26, 31, 52, 80
grades, 89, 96
graduate students, 19
Greece, 121
group work, 117
growth, 59, 120
guidelines, 85

H

hacking, 37
handheld devices, 2, 3, 121
health, 63, 64
hearing impairment, 12
higher education, 3, 7, 42, 75, 84, 91, 93, 94, 95, 100, 103, 108, 109, 112, 120, 121, 127, 128
history, 5, 11, 34, 41, 56
hybrid, 6, 13, 41, 55, 124

I

identification, 52, 83
identity, 46, 72, 99, 124
image, 11, 52, 98, 103
images, 46, 52, 56, 61, 68
improvements, 2, 3, 42, 47, 93, 104
incompatibility, 23
India, 115
Indonesia, 109
industry, 35
information sharing, 48
information technology, 2
infrastructure, 2, 15, 45, 96, 113
institutions, 3, 48, 94, 95, 97
instructional design, 6, 57, 61, 73, 85, 102
integration, 4, 17, 22, 29, 34, 82, 88
integrity, 6, 57, 70, 71, 73, 94, 102
intellectual property, 6, 57, 63, 73, 102
interface, 24, 26, 28, 34, 35, 36, 69, 104
interference, 68, 99
international standards, 67
interoperability, 129
investment, 16
Islam, 108
isolation, 104
Italy, 118, 121

J

Japan, 108
Java, 26, 27, 29, 37, 38, 53, 80, 118
Jordan, 127

K

Korea, 119

L

languages, 24, 30, 32, 69
lead, 46, 49, 55, 66
leadership, 98
learner support, 6, 57, 69, 73
learners, 2, 9, 10, 11, 12, 13, 14, 15, 16, 17, 18, 19, 44, 45, 46, 47, 48, 49, 50, 51, 53, 55, 56, 58, 59, 60, 61, 63, 66, 67, 69, 70, 71, 72, 82, 83, 86, 87, 97, 98, 99, 102, 104, 113, 123
learning, 1, 2, 3, 4, 5, 6, 7, 9, 10, 11, 12, 13, 14, 15, 16, 17, 18, 19, 41, 42, 43, 44, 45, 46, 47, 48, 49, 50, 51, 52, 53, 55, 56, 57, 58, 59, 60, 61, 62, 63, 64, 65, 66, 67, 68, 69, 70, 71, 72, 73, 75, 76, 77, 78, 79, 80, 81, 82, 83, 84, 85, 86, 87, 88, 89, 90, 91, 93, 94, 95, 96, 97, 98, 99, 100, 101, 102, 103, 104, 105, 107, 108, 109, 110, 111, 112, 113, 114, 116, 117, 118, 119, 120, 121, 122, 123, 124, 125, 126, 127, 128, 129
learning activity, 47
learning environment, 10, 11, 16, 43, 48, 59, 75, 81, 91, 97, 102, 112, 117, 122, 126
learning process, 1, 3, 11, 14, 15, 16, 17, 45, 46, 47, 50, 51, 83, 104
learning styles, 50, 55, 56, 124
learning tools, 6, 16, 42, 45, 46, 47, 57, 58, 94, 98, 101
lesson plan, 94
Louisiana, 117

M

Malaysia, 110
management, 15, 24, 27, 36, 68, 94, 114
manipulation, 32
market share, 31, 37
marriage, 11, 55
materials, 2, 11, 12, 13, 15, 16, 17, 18, 44, 46, 47, 50, 53, 55, 56, 61, 79, 84, 89, 94, 99, 102, 104, 114
media, 17, 36, 52, 53, 61, 69, 117
Mediterranean, 128
memory, 23, 27, 33, 53, 61, 68, 72
memory capacity, 53
messages, 13, 95
metaphor, 78
meth, 49, 101
methodology, 81
Microsoft, 24, 29, 30, 31
Middle East, 128
migration, 124
military, 23
MMS, 52
mobile communication, 5, 21, 39, 102
mobile computing, 4, 16, 21, 22, 23, 31, 39, 44, 58, 99, 102, 113, 121
mobile connectivity, 79
mobile device(s), 2, 3, 4, 6, 16, 17, 18, 19, 23, 26, 27, 28, 29, 30, 32, 33, 36, 41, 42, 43, 44, 45, 46, 47, 48, 50, 51, 52, 53, 54, 55, 56, 58, 59, 60, 77, 82, 84, 86, 94, 97, 98, 102, 104, 120, 122, 125, 129
mobile learning, 2, 7, 17, 19, 76, 77, 87, 105, 108, 111, 112, 113, 114, 116, 118, 119, 120, 121, 122, 123, 124, 125, 126, 127, 128, 129
mobile phone, 22, 23, 35, 42, 44, 52, 98, 108, 116, 128
mobile technologies, 7, 9, 17, 18, 19, 42, 44, 45, 47, 48, 58, 75, 79, 83, 87, 95, 97, 98, 99, 102, 111, 119, 122, 127
modelling, 86
models, 6, 12, 23, 54, 57, 61, 73, 102

Index

modifications, 38
modules, 38, 67
motif, 112
motivation, 9, 18, 19, 55, 83, 102
multimedia, 11, 15, 26, 35, 36, 52, 56, 112, 125
music, 22

N

negotiation, 81
Netherlands, 38, 113
networking, 29, 39, 113
New Zealand, 112
next generation, 43, 59, 110

O

online learning, 14, 47, 107, 110, 121
operating system, 4, 12, 23, 24, 26, 27, 28, 29, 30, 31, 32, 35, 36, 37, 38, 39, 55, 67, 101, 102, 114, 115, 116
operations, 28, 64, 68, 69, 96
opportunities, 44, 46, 48
overlap, 79, 80
ownership, 122

P

Pacific, 127
parallel, 29
parents, 13, 95
participants, 10, 95
password, 94
PDAs, 3, 19, 22, 42, 44, 54, 58
personal computers, 16
physical environment, 48
platform, 3, 18, 23, 26, 27, 28, 30, 31, 32, 33, 34, 35, 36, 38, 55, 114, 115, 124
police, 23
policy, 72, 126
population, 43

portability, 5, 21, 22, 45, 67, 83, 102
Portugal, 112
prevention, 72
primary school, 95
principles, 5, 9, 19, 101, 117
problem solving, 83
professionals, 18
profit, 108
programming, 24, 26, 27, 29, 38, 53
programming languages, 53
project, 14, 17, 18, 24, 25, 26, 111, 112, 113
proliferation, 47
propagation, 72
protection, 71
psychology, 108
publishing, 33, 80

Q

quality of service, 82
quantitative technique, 82
quizzes, 94

R

race, 63
radio, 52
reading, 50, 52, 55
reasoning, 83
reception, 50
recognition, 25, 52, 103
reliability, 54, 83
requirements, 4, 5, 6, 7, 11, 18, 22, 33, 50, 57, 59, 60, 61, 62, 63, 64, 67, 70, 71, 72, 73, 75, 78, 79, 82, 83, 87, 88, 90, 93, 94, 96, 100, 101, 102, 103, 122
researchers, 10, 96
resolution, 68, 98, 103
resources, 12, 17, 18, 44, 67, 69, 70, 71, 72, 84, 96, 100
response, 22, 52, 57, 67, 69, 70, 73, 95, 102, 109

restrictions, 59, 61
reusability, 55
rights, 26
risks, 64, 71, 94, 96

S

Samsung, 33, 34, 42, 52, 53, 115
school, 1, 3, 7, 10, 17, 19, 46, 47, 93, 94, 95, 97, 109, 111, 113
school learning, 10
school work, 3
science, 113
scope, 5, 68, 81
secondary schools, 94, 100, 103
security, 6, 27, 35, 36, 54, 57, 63, 70, 71, 72, 73, 94, 96, 99, 102, 105
sensing, 34
sensors, 18, 24, 34, 46, 52, 86
servers, 45, 95, 97
service provider, 54
service quality, 66
services, 14, 15, 16, 34, 36, 44, 58, 60, 65, 66, 67, 71, 77, 78, 83, 86, 88, 95, 96, 99, 113
shape, 35
simulation, 96
Singapore, 122
skimming, 50
smart phones, 22
SMS, 39, 52
SNS, 34
sociability, 57, 73, 102
social construct, 43, 79
social constructivism, 79
social interactions, 79
social learning, 61
social network, 34, 95, 115
socialization, 63
society, 42, 84, 99
software, 5, 12, 13, 17, 21, 22, 23, 24, 26, 27, 30, 32, 36, 37, 39, 55, 58, 60, 65, 66, 67, 70, 71, 72, 83, 95, 96, 100, 102, 105, 115, 124, 125, 126
solution, 32, 36, 114
South Africa, 113, 118, 123
Spain, 128
spam, 71
specifications, 31
speech, 12, 51
speed of response, 6
spyware, 71
stakeholders, 50
standardization, 124
state, 15, 69, 128
statistics, 111
storage, 25, 33, 38, 55, 67, 71
structure, 50, 55, 61
structuring, 83
style, 50, 120
Sun, 37
supervision, 14
Sweden, 108, 112, 120, 121, 122
Switzerland, 114
synthesis, 83

T

tablets, 31, 115
Taiwan, 108, 112, 113
target, 17, 23, 31, 61, 64, 72, 81
teachers, 2, 10, 77, 94, 95, 104
technical support, 2
techniques, 4, 10, 46, 49, 50, 51, 68, 101, 114
technologies, 2, 3, 7, 9, 11, 12, 15, 17, 18, 19, 23, 32, 36, 42, 44, 45, 46, 47, 48, 54, 55, 58, 59, 75, 77, 79, 83, 87, 95, 97, 98, 99, 102, 104, 111, 112, 119, 122, 127
technology, 2, 3, 4, 5, 9, 11, 13, 15, 17, 19, 22, 42, 43, 44, 45, 54, 55, 59, 77, 79, 80, 88, 97, 98, 99, 100, 101, 108, 109, 111, 113, 116, 117, 119, 120, 123, 127
telecommunications, 35
teleconferencing, 12

Index

telephones, 52, 80
temperature, 114
tenants, 67
term plans, 98
tertiary education, 122
testing, 112
text messaging, 24, 52
textbooks, 10, 11, 15
theft, 72
tics, 19, 47, 73
trade, 35
trainees, 10
training, 7, 12, 15, 18, 44, 48, 49, 93, 94, 96, 97, 100, 103, 105, 118, 119, 123, 127
transactions, 63
transformation, 111
transformations, 24
translation, 58
transmission, 15, 22
transparency, 29
tunneling, 71
tutoring, 14, 118

U

United Kingdom (UK), 94, 107, 109, 110, 111, 112, 114, 116, 118, 123, 126
United States (USA), 42, 107, 108, 109, 110, 114, 115, 117, 118, 119, 120, 123, 124, 125
universities, 2, 3, 95
updating, 50
user data, 71

V

variables, 10
vehicles, 23
videos, 52, 94
vision, 12, 34, 42
visualization, 96
vocabulary, 58
vulnerability, 36

W

Washington, 108, 109, 119, 120, 123
water, 110
web, 3, 6, 12, 15, 32, 36, 37, 41, 53, 54, 55, 80, 95, 121, 124
web browser, 3, 12, 54, 80
web pages, 3
web service, 37
websites, 53, 54, 55, 94
windows, 29, 30, 116
wireless connectivity, 58
wireless devices, 42, 44
wireless networks, 22
wireless technology, 58, 120
Wisconsin, 120
workers, 3

X

XML, 54, 55